Craftwork Techniques
Of The Native Americans

Revised & Expanded Second Edition

Craftwork Techniques

Second Edition

Published by:
Crazy Crow Trading Post, LLC
P.O. Box 847
Pottsboro, TX 75076
(903) 786-2287
www.crazycrow.com

Cover Beadwork by:
Scott Sutton

Edited by:
John Durnian, J. Rex Reddick,
Jessica Reddick Gatlin

Designed by:
Michael Catellier, J. Rex Reddick

Illustrations & Photographs by:
Scott Sutton, Michael Catellier

ISBN 1-929572-34-4
(Previously ISBN 1-929572-29-8)

© Copyright 2014, 2019 by Crazy Crow Trading Post, LLC
All Rights Reserved. No part of this publication may be reproduced or transmitted in any form or by any means, electronic or mechanical, including photocopying, recording or any information storage and retrieval system, without written permission from publisher.

Published 2019
First Edition published 2014. Second Edition 2019.
Printed in the United States of America

Introduction

After the success of my first book, **Beadwork Techniques of the Native Americans**, I began to recognize a need for a second book that would go a step further and include full details on how to make projects that were not previously covered.

This volume provides complete, step-by-step instructions for eight contemporary projects. Each is described in detail, with full-color photographs outlining each phase of construction. Information includes the selection of materials and required supplies. Close-up photos show how each step is accomplished, thus helping the reader to develop skills necessary to produce other items similar to these.

Because the various beadwork techniques for these projects has been covered in my earlier work, as well as in many others, this version concentrates on the construction methods and materials that I use today, along with many tips and techniques that I have learned or developed and found successful over the years.

It is my hope that the information presented here will inspire you to create many beautiful objects and give you hours of pleasure while pursuing the craft of beadwork.

Contents

1. Materials   7
2. Medallions   9
3. Belt Buckles   19
4. Barrettes   27
5. Loom Beaded Belts   37
6. Scalp Feathers   47
7. Flat Fan   59
8. Small Dance Bag   79
9. Moccasins   87

Materials

Chapter One
Materials

Detailed instructions for appliqué, lazy stitch and edge beadwork can be found in my book, ***Beadwork Techniques of the Native Americans,*** and these are used for the projects outlined in this book. The basic tools, materials and supplies required for these items are discussed here, with any supplies unique to the individual projects being detailed at the beginning of each chapter.

Scissors: Two types of scissors are most useful: the small, sharp type used for crafts or embroidery, and those with a knife-edge, made by Gingher, which are a good choice as they are high quality and will last a lifetime.

Leather Punch: The best type is the kind with an adjustable wheel that will punch several different sizes of holes.

Awl: A sharp awl is handy for use with a number of different beading projects.

Embroidery Hoops: These hoops are available in both wood and plastic; however, I always use plastic hoops because the wooden hoops do not hold the work tightly enough. I recommend using one of the plastic hoops which has a ridge, or lip, on one side of the inner ring. This ridge should always be oriented on the top edge when securing the backing.

Backing Materials: Hospital sheeting, which is also known as baby crib sheets, is preferable for backing as it is tightly woven and holds the work well. Heavy craft paper can be obtained from grocery sacks or purchased at an office supply store. Grid or graph paper purchased at office supply stores is useful for keeping lines straight and designs proportional.

Drawing Tools: A compass or circle template is necessary for drawing circles when making rosettes, and a ruler is useful for drawing straight lines.

Beading Needles: English made "Sharps" needles in size 11 or 12 work well for this type of work depending on bead size. Size 11 is normally used for 11/0 beads and size 12 is used for 12/0 beads. 12 sharps needles can also be used with 13/0 cut beads.

Thread: Nylon thread sold under the brand name "Nymo" is excellent for many crafts and beadwork. It is available in several sizes, and size "D" is usually the best for the projects described here. If very small beads are used, size "A" or "B" should be used.

Beeswax: Coating thread with beeswax prevents tangling and extends the life of the thread. Select pure beeswax as opposed to products containing paraffin.

Glue: Aleene's Tacky Glue is an excellent choice for gluing leather and cloth. It is available from most craft and hobby suppliers.

Beads: Czech "cut" beads in size 11/0 or 13/0 are preferred for this type of work. Other types such as 3-cuts, silver-lined or regular seed beads can also be used. Since barrettes and belt buckles often contain a circular section, the same size beads should be used in order to keep the circle uniform. This is also true for geometric designs done in the free style. When doing floral designs, one can mix different sizes and types of beads to create pleasing effects.

Medallions

Materials - Tools & Supplies

- Scissors - Gingher is an excellent brand
- Embroidery hoops - Assorted sizes
- Backing - Hospital sheeting, sometimes known as baby crib sheets. An alternative back ing material is Peltex 70-Pellon Ultra Firm Stabilizer, which is a type of inner facing.
- Paper
- Compass or circular protractor
- Pencils or pens
- Ruler
- Size 11 or 12 needles
- Size D Nymo thread
- Beeswax
- Aleene's Tacky Glue
- Size 11/0 or 13/0 cut seed beads

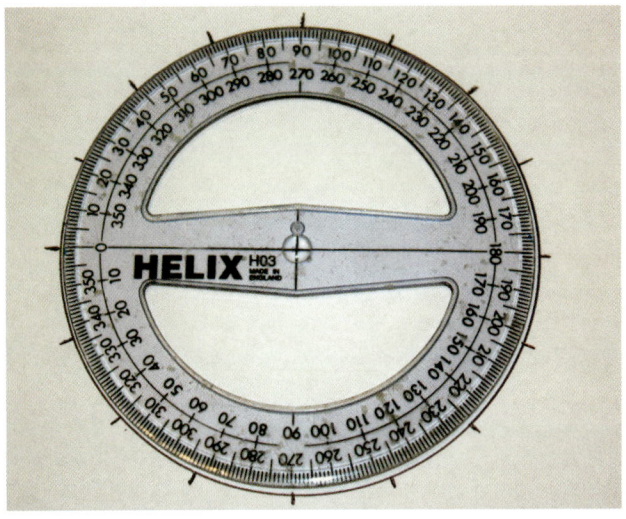

Chapter Two
Medallions

The appliqué beadwork technique has many uses in the creation of Native American craft projects. Some projects that use this technique are medallions, beaded aprons, skirts, shirts, blankets, etc., some of which are made in floral patterns or abstract shapes. This technique was employed by many tribes throughout North America. Medallions are usually round and are used on a variety of projects such as necklaces, bustle centers, purses, otter draggers, hair ties and a wide assortment of other craft projects.

This chapter provides step-by-step directions for creating a medallion, including layout and design, as well as the appliqué beadwork technique itself and how to put the entire project together.

Getting Started

As shown in the photo at left, place a circular protractor on your paper and trace around the outside edge. Mark equal increments around the circle. The photo shows an example that I use. This is divided at 22.5 degree increments which results in 16 divisions. Mark 22.5, 45, 67.5, 90 and so on until you get to 360. This will create the even number of 16 pie-shaped sections. Marking 15 degree increments will create 18 divisions, resulting in the odd number of 9 sections. There is actually no right or wrong number here, so you may lay this out using whatever number you choose.

Craftwork Techniques

Using a ruler, connect the marks across the circle to create grid lines. These grid lines will help keep your work even and straight. If a compass was used to create the circle, it is still necessary to mark increments and connect the marks. Either way, you will end up with a fully gridded circle. Hint: Use this as a master and make copies!

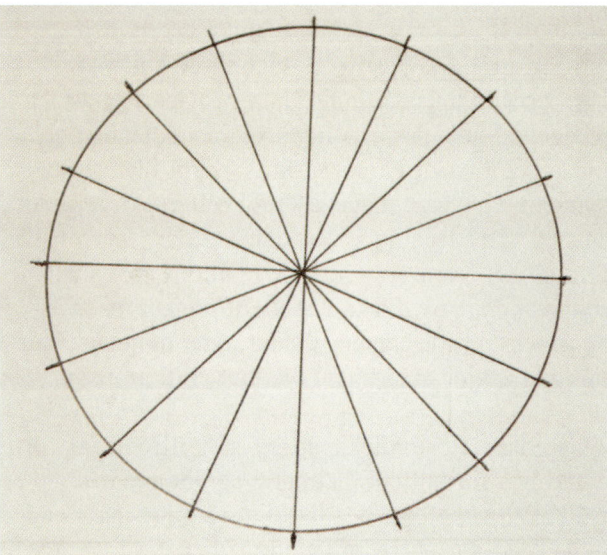

Next, we need to put the gridded paper and backing on the embroidery hoops in order to provide a stable base on which to bead. On most plastic embroidery hoops, the smaller hoop has a ridge on one side. Place the smaller hoop on a flat surface with the ridge up. Put the backing material and paper pattern over the top of the hoop. Open the larger hoop almost entirely and place it over the top as shown above.

Push the outer hoop down until it is completely around the bottom hoop. The paper and backing should be between the two hoops and held securely in place.

Note that the top hoop is under the ridge of the bottom hoop.

10

Medallions

Back

Ready to work on!

View of the back with the top hoop secured.

Tighten the screw until the backing and paper are firmly secured. Sometimes it is necessary to pull the backing and paper towards the area where the screw is located. This helps to keep the paper and backing smooth and taut before the embroidery hoop is tightened.

Trim the paper and backing around the hoop with sharp scissors.

Editor's Note: Some beadworkers do not use embroidery hoops. Instead, they use Peltex inner facing and paper that is stapled together, usually in a square.

Before starting the beadwork, it is necessary to have an understanding about color and design. Most Indian made beadwork uses combinations of contrasting colors, which make the designs stand out. Colors can compliment each other, but there must be contrast as well. For example, dark red next to light red will work, but dark green next to black will not. The black and dark green blend together and the design will not stand out. Traditional Indian beadwork often used primary colors, and this could have been due to the fact that there was a limited choice of bead colors. However, this is not the case today, with most trading posts offering beads in a range of over fifty colors. Bead sample cards are available from most trading posts, and it is a good idea for the beginning beadworker to purchase some of these to see the vast color choices that are available.

One needs to go to a big powwow and look around to see all the beautiful work that is done in every color you can imagine. Another consideration is the use of different types of beads. In doing medallions (rosettes), a beginning beadworker should use beads of equal size. In curvilinear floral or abstract style work, bead sizes can be mixed. Some magnificent work can be created on aprons, blankets, skirts and other items mixing iris beads and cut beads in both transparent and opaque colors, and the effect is quite beautiful!

Now let's talk about designs, which is always a tough subject! I've always made medallions thinking about the background color before I start to bead. I understand that not everyone is born to be an artist and

Craftwork Techniques

when beginning we need some guidelines. If you are a beginning beadworker, it is advisable to keep your designs simple. This chapter contains a fairly simple, yet pleasing, design; however, some designs can become very complicated, especially on larger medallions. The way the grid is laid out (12 sections, 16 sections, 18 sections etc.) will dictate how complicated the design can be. A number of sections that is divisible by two makes the most uniform designs. Geometric shapes such as blocks, triangles, and points will help with building designs. Feather designs and bands of color can also be incorporated into your design elements.

When first starting, if you need to have a pattern, you can simply draw one or two sections on the background paper. Then, the rest of the design will be repeated. Use the grid lines as your guide for the remainder of the medallion as they are a key factor in this style of beadwork. As you will see later in this chapter, always make the design hit the grid lines and work the background around the design. Later, as you become more proficient, you will start to use the gridlines alone to do the work.

Using size "D" Nymo thread, cut the end at an angle, which helps in threading the needle. Next, thread the first needle and pull the thread through leaving a tail. We will call this the single threaded needle. Thread the second needle and pull the thread through so that the ends are even (the double threaded needle). Wax both threads with beeswax, but not too heavily. Knot both threads using an overhand, or sewer's knot. Wrap the thread around your finger, roll it off and pull the knot down.

Using a double thread, bring the needle up 1/2 bead width away from center.

With one bead on your thread, go down on the opposite side of the center point.

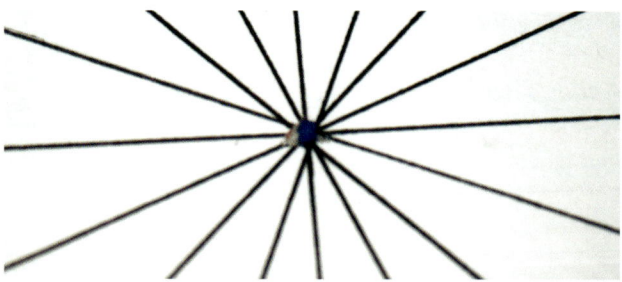

The center bead is now in place.

Still using the double threaded needle, bring it up 1/2 bead width from the center bead. Place 7 beads on this needle. Hold the thread at a 90° angle to the center bead. Bring the single threaded needle up on the outside of the double thread.

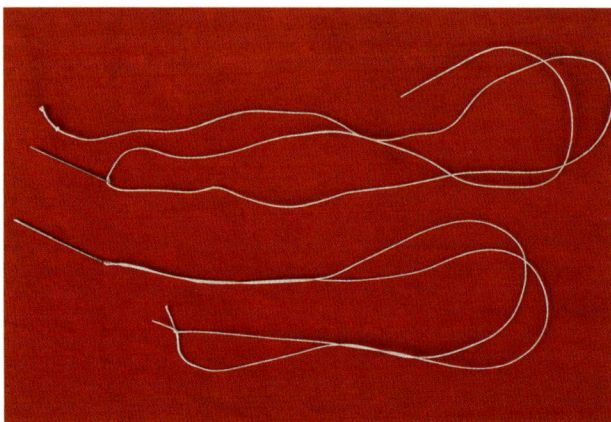

Above: *Single threaded needle (one side of the thread is longer than the other with a knot in the end).*
Below: *Double threaded needle (both sides of the thread are the same length and knotted together).*

12

Medallions

Sew down on other side of double thread, catching the double thread with the stitch.

End this row as you did the first one by going through the first bead with the double threaded needle and then down through backing.

To sew the last bead in place, go through the first bead with the double threaded needle again and then down through backing.

Begin the third row in the same way as the second row except now sew down between every second bead using the single thread.

The first row is now complete. Start the second row by coming up with the double threaded needle 1/2 bead width away from the first row.

Continue around the row, sewing between every two beads and keeping the double thread at a 90° angle as shown above.

Begin stitching this row down as you did for the first row. Stitch between each bead with the single threaded needle, keeping double threaded needle at 90° to the first row.

End this row as you did the first two. When starting the fourth row, design will be added so it is important where you bring the double threaded needle up. Come up a 1/2 bead width away from the previous row and 1 bead width from a "spoke" on the backing.

13

Craftwork Techniques

Note that each pink (light colored) bead is stitched so that it falls on one of the grid lines.

In this view you can see that the white beads are stitched so that they lay on the grid lines while the number of green beads in the background is somewhat flexible. Some spaces have two beads and some have three, but the most important thing is that each white bead falls exactly on a grid line. If there is a little extra space between the beads, it is okay. This is much better than packing too many beads into a row.

The feather elements are now complete at this point, with each feather lining up correctly on a grid line.

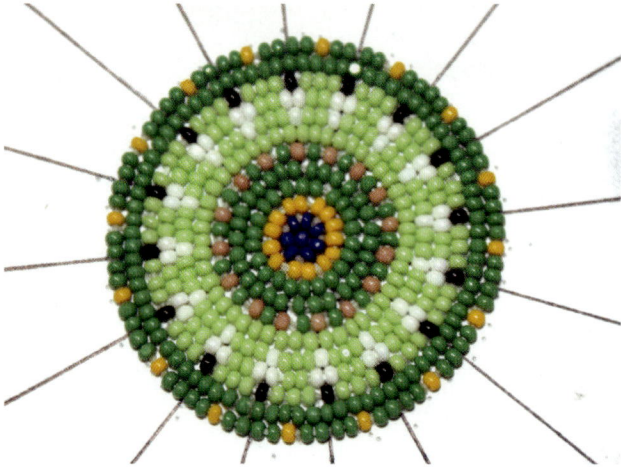

As this design continues, I'm using imaginary grid lines between those I have drawn. This allows for options that can be incorporated into the design.

The basic medallion is now completed. Note that the points once again fall on the grid lines.

Cut the medallion from the hoops.

14

Medallions

Apply glue to the reverse side.

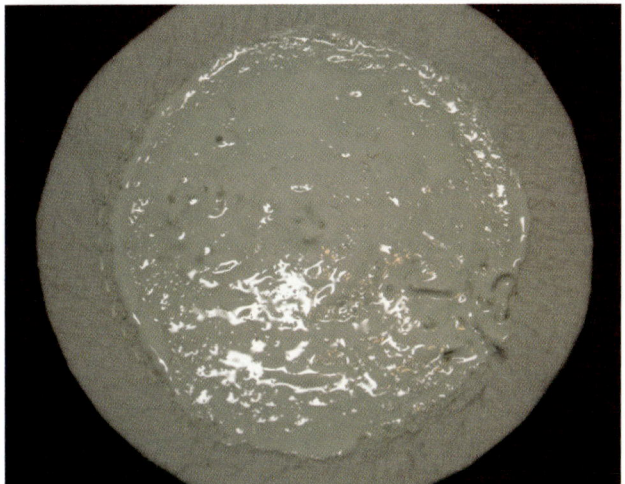

Spread a thin coat of glue over the entire area, covering all the stitching.

Press the medallion onto the buckskin backing.

Trim around the medallion using a pair of sharp scissors and cutting as close as possible to the beadwork but being careful not to cut any of the threads.

Side view after trimming.

The next step in the process is doing the edgework. Two types of edge beading can be used here: Picot ("turtle stitch") beadwork or whip stitch edging. Northern-style beadwork often employs the whip stitch, while picot edge beading is usually found on Southern-style medallions.

The whip stitch requires a little wider edge on the backing material, so it is necessary to leave about 1/8" to 1/4" around the edge when trimming the medallion. This varies depending on how wide you want to make the band of beadwork. For instructions on this technique, see the next chapter on making belt buckles.

For the example we are making here, the picot style of beading is used and is explained in detail.

15

Craftwork Techniques

With your needle double threaded and knotted, insert it from the back toward the front of the medallion and exiting beside the outer row of beads.

String 3 beads...

Insert the needle about a bead width (standing on end) up from the back to the front as you did for the first stitch.

Then go back through the 3rd bead with the needle directed toward the second bead. Now we will begin adding 2 beads at a time.

Put two more beads on the needle and make a a stitch just like the second one you made. Then go back up through the second bead with the needle pointed towards the first bead.

This gives the noted "turtle" appearance of the work. Two flat beads with one in between standing on end. This forms the lace pattern, or "picot" edge.

If you run out of thread, start another one. Here's how. Put on two more beads as usual, stitching from the front to the back, but don't go back through the second bead yet.

Medallions

Cut the thread off and rethread your needle with a longer piece. Enter the backing about one stitch away, comimg up where the first thread ends, but don't knot it yet.

Run your needle through the backing and tie an overhand knot. Go through the backing again and then through the loop of thread. Pull this taught and repeat.

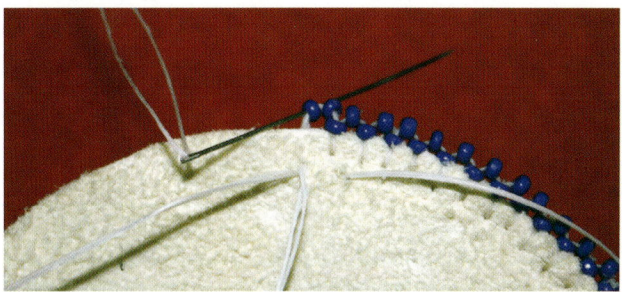

Go up through the second bead with the needle pointing towards the first bead.

Back view of the finished medallion back. Note the evenness of the stitches which makes a uniform edge.

After pulling the thread almost all the way through and leaving a short end, tie a knot with this and the end of your last thread, pulling both ends snug!

Finished Medallion

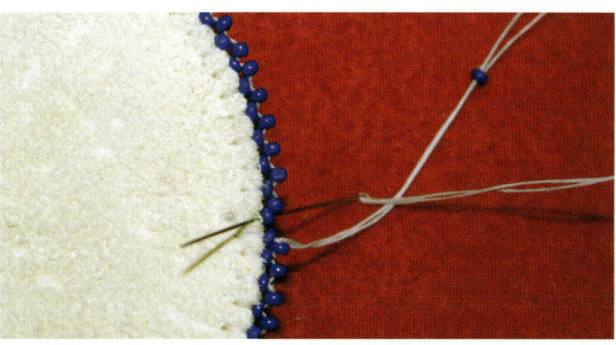

For the last stitch, put one bead on the needle. Go back down through the very first bead that was stitched on.

That completes a simple medallion which can be used for many purposes. You are now on your way to becoming an accomplished bead worker, so keep practicing!

Chapter Three

Belt Buckles

Materials - Tools & Supplies

Proper tools and materials are essential to the success of any project, as discussed in the first chapter. The following items are required for this project but will also be useful for most of the other beadwork that you will do in the future.

- Craft Scissors
- Gingher Shears
- Embroidery Hoops
- Hospital Sheeting
- Gridded Paper
- Compass or Circle Template & Ruler
- Beading Needles
- D Nymo Thread

Additional Materials

Leather Backing: Any type can be used for the finished product but do not use vinyl or felt as they do not look good and will not hold up to wear as well as genuine leather.

Beads: I prefer 11/0 cut beads but other sizes, such as 13/0, and types can be used. Keep in mind that all the same size beads must be used in order to keep the circular pattern uniform. If using floral designs in the free style, different sizes or types of beads can be mixed. Geometric designs should also be done using beads of the same size.

This project takes the reader step-by-step through the construction of a beaded belt buckle. The beadwork techniques required here are discussed in detail in my book, ***Beadwork Techniques of the Native Americans***, as well as in the preceding chapter on medallions, so I will not go through each step again. Detailed suggestions and examples are provided which demonstrate the blending of a circular style medallion with the free style.

In making buckles, several beadwork techniques can be used in conjunction with one another, thus allowing a wide variety of styles and designs. One of the most versatile types of beadwork is appliqué, and in this style, there are two types: free style used in geometric and floral work and circular style as used in medallions. So, in making a belt buckle, either style or a combination of both can be used.

Craftwork Techniques

To get started, the first thing to do is plan the shape and design of the buckle. You might choose from floral, geometric, circular, or a combination of these styles, as in this demonstration piece. For this buckle, the center will be a circular design and the outside will be a geometric design. **See Figure 1.**

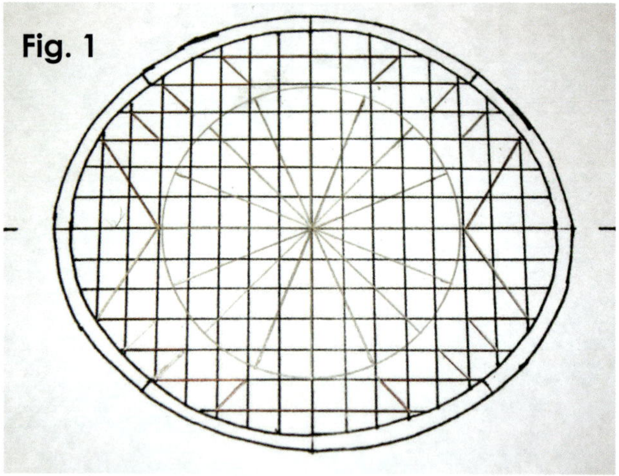

Fig. 1

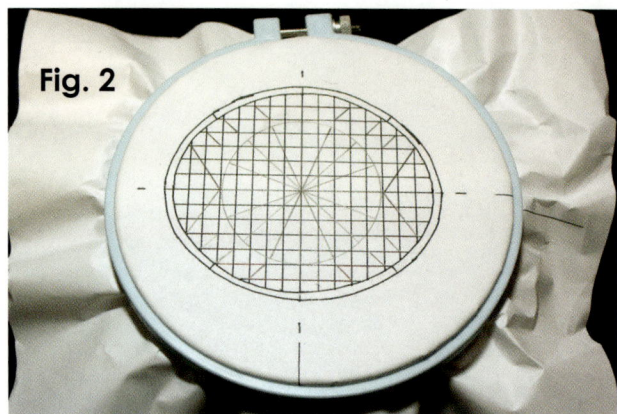

Fig. 2

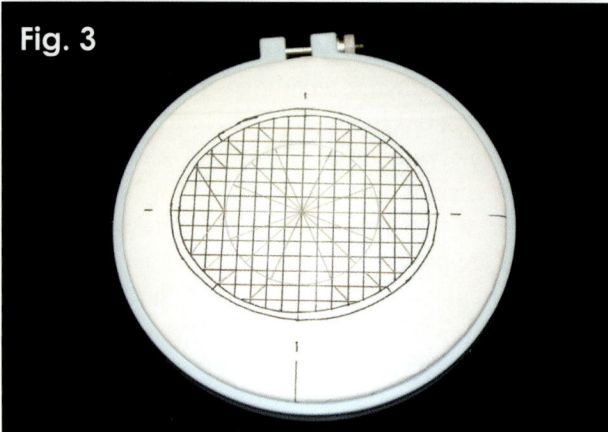

Fig. 3

In planning your design for a metal buckle blank, it is very important to allow approximately a 1/8" extra border around the outside edge of the backing material. This allows for easier edge beading to be done when completing the buckle.

The actual pattern should be on a fairly heavy paper, such as that used for computers, as a thin sheet will tear too easily. After drawing your design, place it in the embroidery hoops as shown, along with the backing material. Make sure the piece is as taut as you can get it, taking care not to tear the paper. Tightening the hoops slowly will help snug up the fabric and paper together. **See Figures 2 & 3.**

For this buckle, we are using a silver colored spot in the center. In order to place the spot, it is necessary to pre-cut two tiny slits in the backing to put the prongs through. To secure them in place, the prongs are simply folded inward on themselves. I use a blade such as a scalpel or an X-Acto® knife to make these cuts. **Figure 4** shows a series of photos which show the placement of the spot. Although this is not required, it is an option that can be used which is decorative as well as helpful in creating a nice round, even first row of beads.

Fig. 4

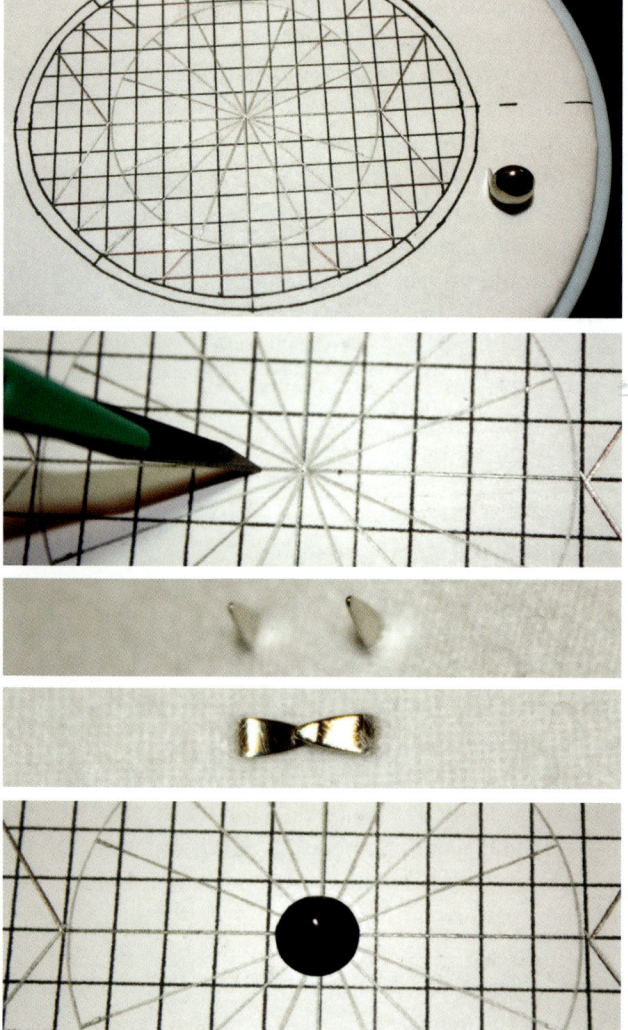

20

Now that the backing is prepared, the beadwork panel can be made. First, the circular section in the center will be done, followed by the outer border, then the geometric outlines, and finally, the fill-in of the geometric portion. This will complete the beadwork panel as shown in **Figures 5 - 8**.

Fig. 5

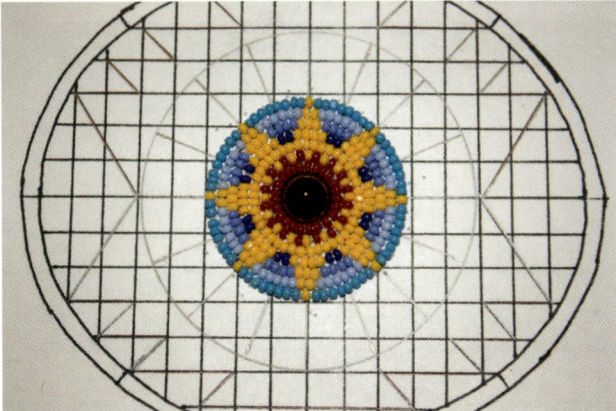

Note that the design follows the guide lines.

Fig. 6

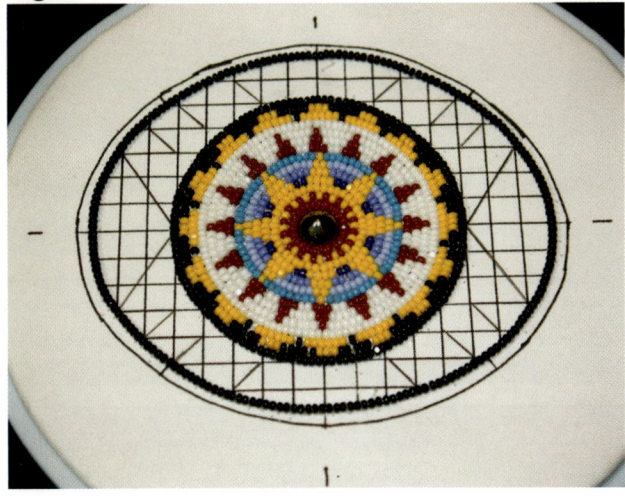

Fig. 7

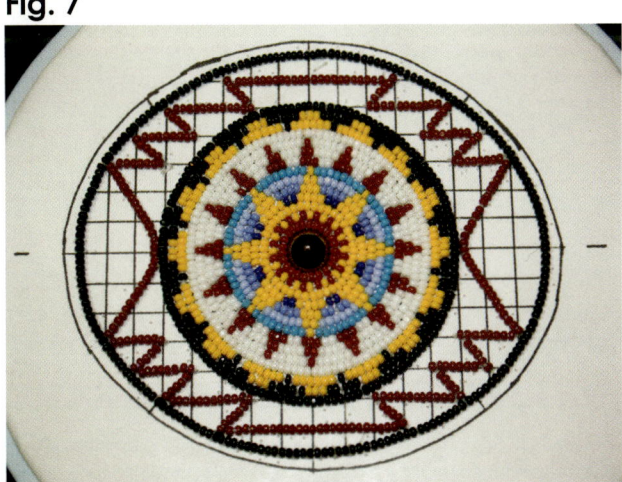

Note: It is very important to have the outer row of a geometric design completed in order to provide a boundary, or border, when filling in a background area. Do not attempt to bead the panel and then try to surround it with the outside row, as it will not have the neat, "clean" look that is so important in quality work. This outer row should be sewn down between every two beads. After these borders are completed, the background can be filled in to complete the panel.

Fig. 8

Spread a thin, even coating of glue over the entire back surface of the beadwork panel and then press it firmly onto the buckle blank, making sure that it is centered from side-to-side and from top-to-bottom. **See Figure 9**. Also, be aware of the orientation of the design, as some designs, such as pictorials, have a top and bottom and should be placed accordingly.

Fig. 9

Craftwork Techniques

Orientation is important, and men's buckles are made so that when worn, they buckle from the left, with the bar on the left and the pin on the right. Women's buckles are made in reverse, with the bar on the right and the pin on the left so they buckle from the right.

Fig. 10

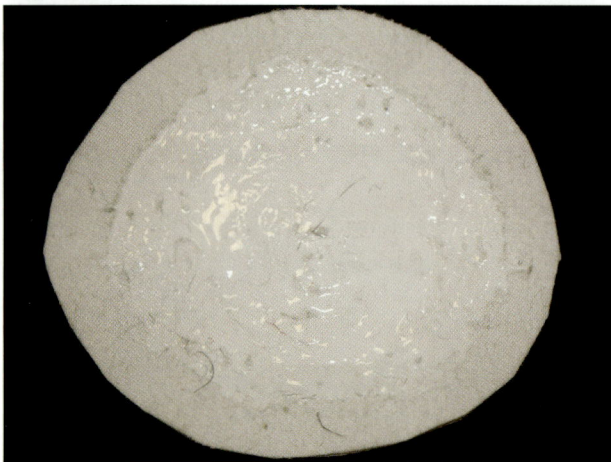

Fig. 11

The next step is to attach the leather backing. Cut a piece of leather allowing approximately 1/4" of overlap around the edges of the buckle. See **Figures 12 & 14**. The excess leather will eventually be trimmed off when the buckle is finished. Press this solid piece of leather down on the back of the buckle. This will help to locate where to punch the hole for the buckle pin. Punch a hole for the pin using a hole punch or leather punch. Place the leather over the backing to locate the position of the two holes to be punched for the belt bar. Once the holes are punched, cut slits in the leather from the outside toward each of the holes. See **Figure 12**.

Spread glue evenly over the back of the metal buckle blank. Starting with the pin, place the leather on the buckle and smooth it out, working it towards the buckle bar. When you reach the bar, work the leather under it and, working it so that it lays smooth and flat, make sure the slits are pulled back together. See **Figures 13-15**.

Fig. 12

Fig. 13

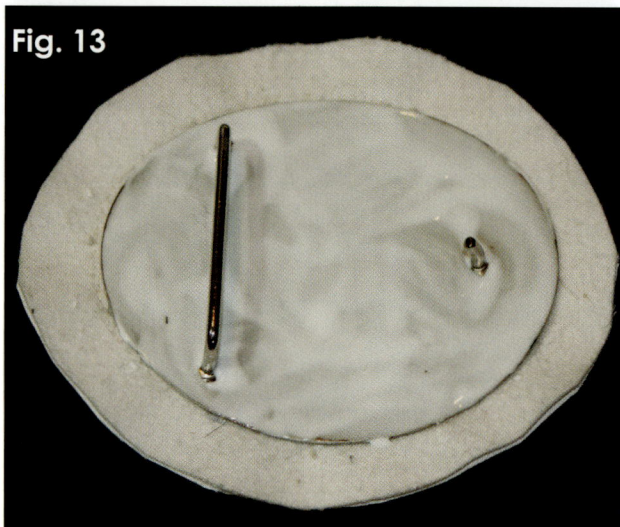

22

Belt Buckles

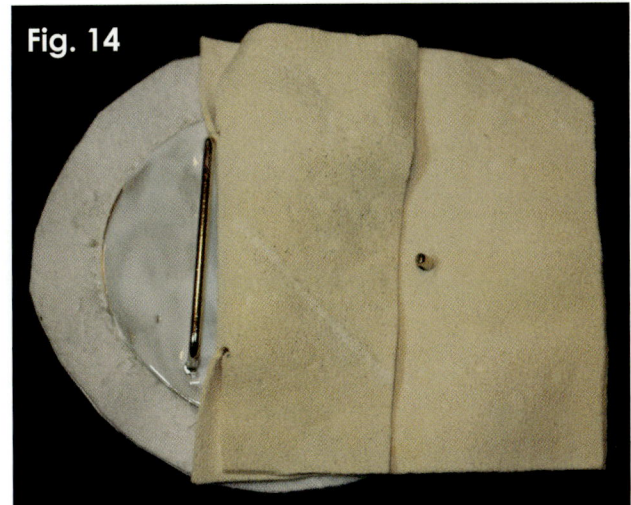

Fig. 14

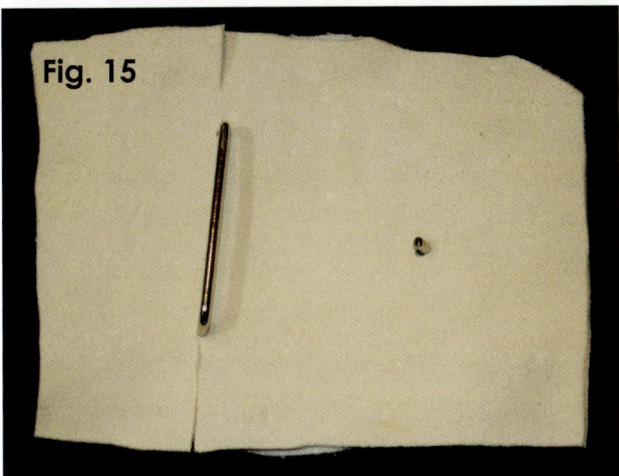

Fig. 15

Trim the leather and paper backing with sharp scissors, leaving a 1/8 inch edge around the entire buckle. Make this cut as smooth as possible, avoiding any ragged edges. See **Figures 16 & 17**.

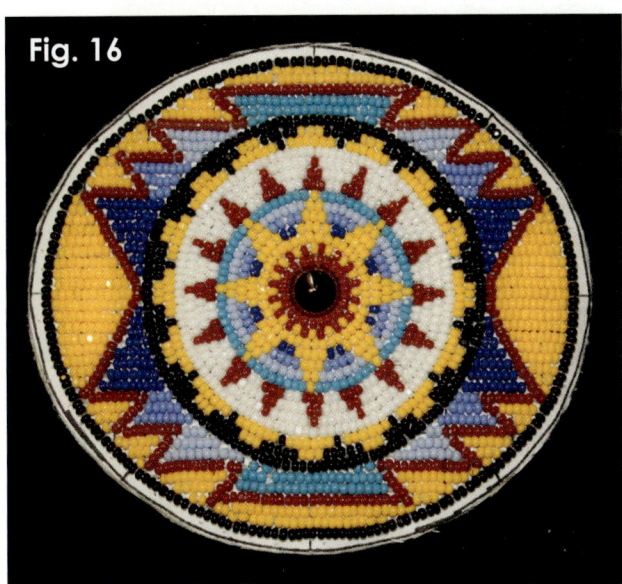

Fig. 16

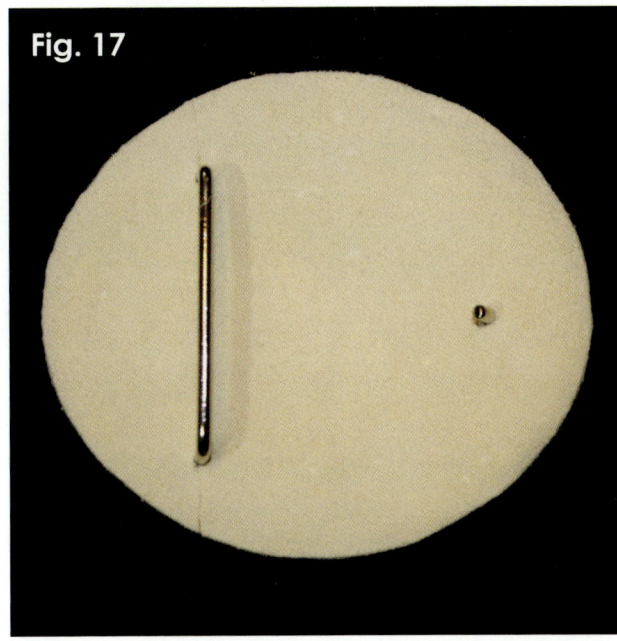

Fig. 17

The next step is adding a beaded edging around the buckle. Begin with a double threaded needle with a tight overhand knot at the end. This work may be started anywhere along the edge, but I recommend starting at the top center of the buckle. The stitch used here is a whip stitch, as shown in **Figure 18**.

Fig. 18

23

Craftwork Techniques

Fig. 19

Bands of different colors may be used or you may choose to use a single color. To ensure that these bands of colors are spaced evenly, markings may be placed along the edge to use as a reference before the work is started.

If the thread becomes too short to continue beading, simply weave it in and out of the backing where the whip stitching will be continued. Then start a new thread just like the first one. The needle is inserted from the back side of the buckle between the last two rows of beadwork, as shown in **Figure 20**, below.

Fig. 20

Belt Buckles

Fig. 21

Continue the beadwork around the edge until you reach the beginning. **Figure 21** shows both a front and back view of the finished buckle.

25

Barrettes

Chapter Four

Barrettes

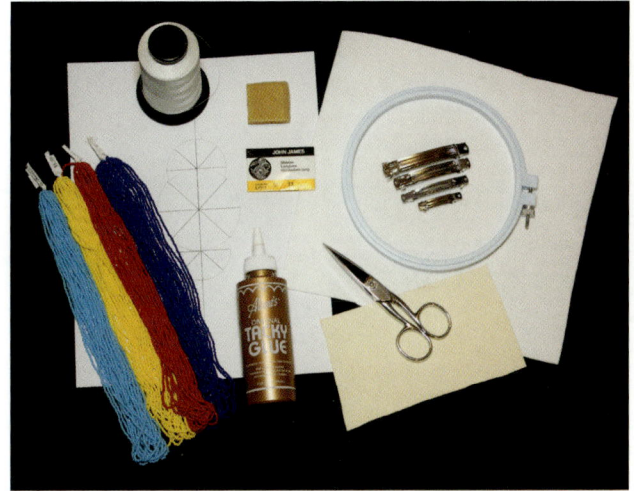

Materials

In addition to the basic materials discussed in Chapter One, the following tools and supplies are required for this project.

▶ **Beads:** 11/0 cuts are my favorite, but 13/0 cuts, iris and other types of glass beads can be used.

▶ **Leather:** Any type of leather can be used for backing the final product, but materials such as vinyl or felt should be avoided as they just do not look good on the finished piece.

▶ **Barrette Hardware:** These are available from craft supply stores in several different sizes and types. The ones made in France are usually better quality.

▶ **Pattern:** I do not use a fully detailed pattern, but rather guidelines (or a template) of what I want to create. Several styles are presented below. The actual pattern should be drawn on fairly heavy paper, as a thin sheet will tear easily.

Barrettes are one of the projects I most enjoy creating. Possible variations in shape, size, colors and designs are almost limitless. Just when you think you have seen them all, someone comes out with a new style! The beadwork techniques for these are typically appliqué and edge beading and this chapter covers details of layout, colors and designs.

Before You Begin

First of all, you should give some thought to how you want the finished barrette to look. What color do you want to be dominant? In this example I have chosen to use blue as the predominant color, with a light blue as the primary background color. One of the keys to nice appliqué work is to use contrasting colors that "pop" when placed next to one another. Avoid using rainbow patterns that are, for example, three shades of red. These will not be easily distinguishable from even a short distance away, and in a case like this, all you would see is a large area of red! The more experience you have with beading the easier this will become. If you cannot visualize your design, you can draw it out and color it in using colored pencils. *Hint:* Since there are 8 sections to the center part, you only need to draw out one section and repeat it around the rest of the sections.

Patterns

There are almost as many styles, shapes and sizes of patterns possible for barrettes as there are ideas in one's head! The templates pictured here are some of the ones that I often use and any of these will allow you to create a beautiful barrette like the ones shown in the accompanying photos.

27

Craftwork Techniques

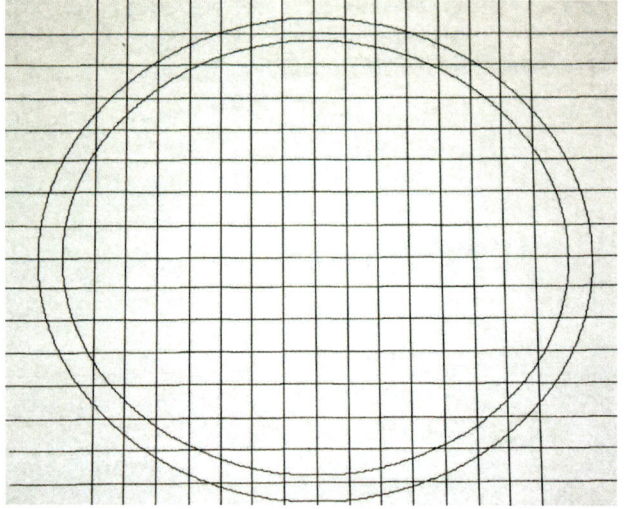

Oval Barrette for Geometric or Floral Designs

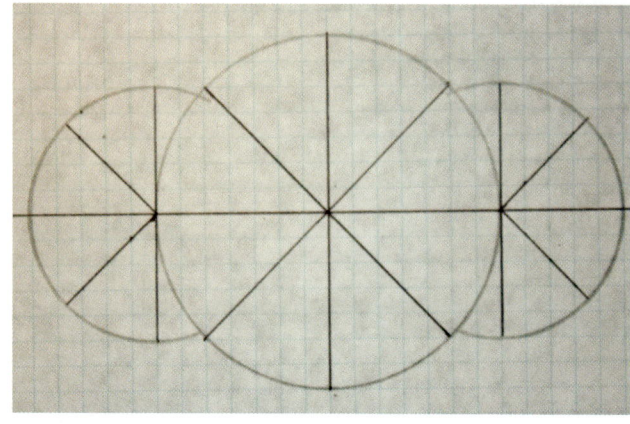

Large & Small Circular Barrette

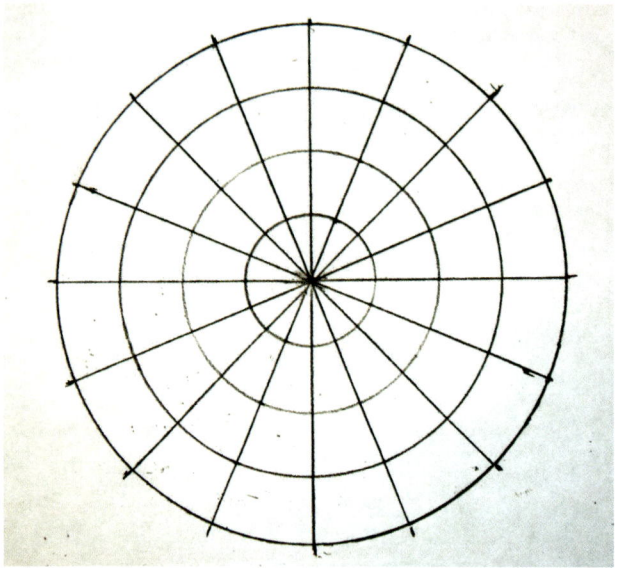

Circular Barrette

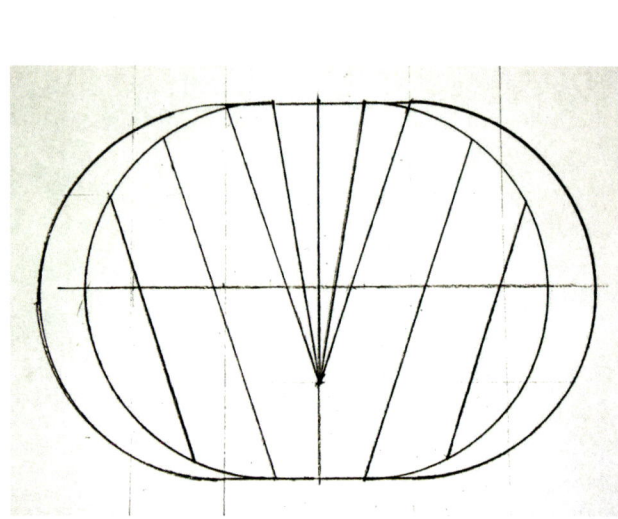

Waterbird Barrette

Rose & Feather Barrette

 Barrettes

Geometric Barrette

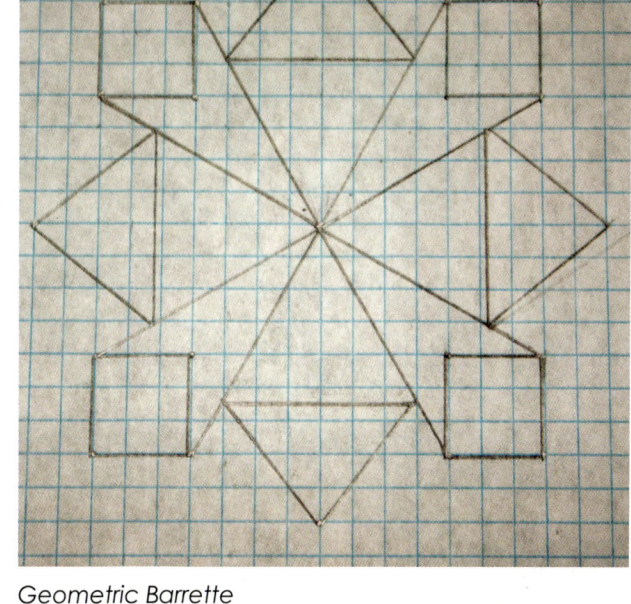
Geometric Barrette

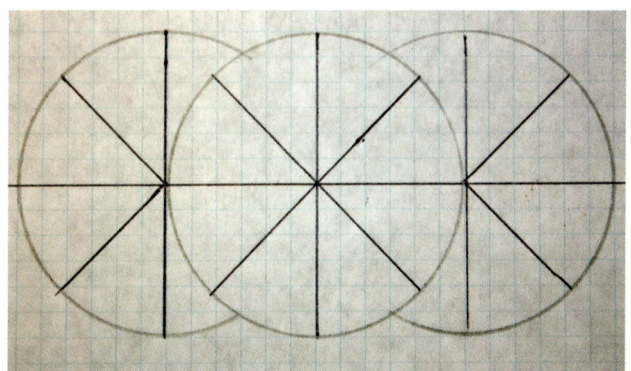
3 Large Circles Barrette

Geometric Barrette

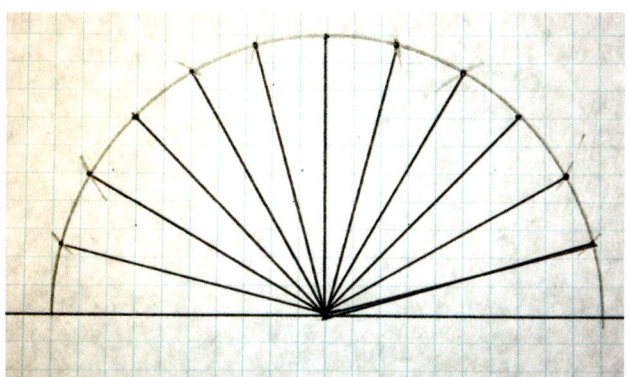
Half-Circle Barrette

Craftwork Techniques

Any of the templates on pages 28 and 29 could be used to create beautiful barrettes like the ones in the photos shown here.

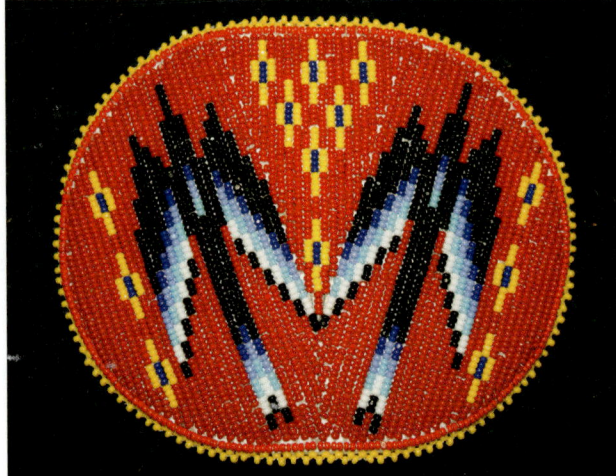

Waterbird Barrette

Geometric Barrette

Half-Circle Barrette

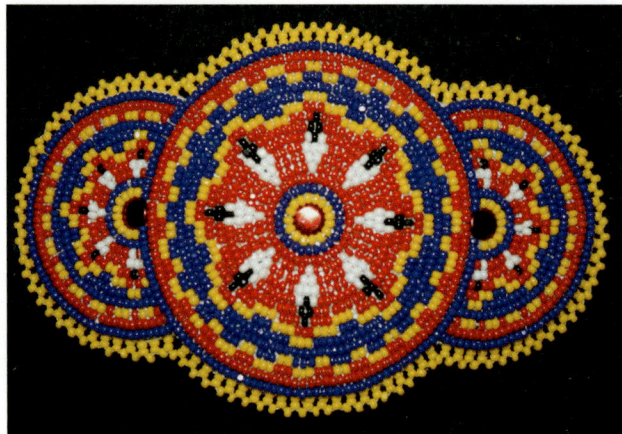

Large & Small Circular Barrette

Large & Small Circular Barrette

Getting Started

For this barrette, I have chosen to use a "large and small circle" style template. A few of the techniques for appliqué work will be covered, but a review of the appliqué technique in the chapter on medallions will be beneficial if you are not already familiar with this. The next step is to secure the backing and pattern in the embroidery hoop. Place the inner ring on a hard surface with the lip side up. Most plastic embroidery hoops have this lip or ridge on one side of the inner ring, and it should always be on the top edge when placing the backing on it. If you put wrong side up, it can cause the work to slip. Wooden hoops generally do not hold the work tightly enough, so I use the plastic hoops, which hold much better.

Lay the backing material on the hoop, followed by the paper template. Then, after opening the screw of the outer hoop most of the way, place it over the template, backing and inner hoop. Start to tighten the

Barrettes

screw while working the outer hoop over the ridge of the inner hoop. Continue to tighten the screw, securing the layers of both the backing and the template firmly in the hoops. See **Figure 1** which illustrates how the tightened hoop should look. Now you can trim off the excess backing material so it will not be in the way while beading.

Fig. 1

When using round templates, there are a couple of options for starting the beadwork. The first is to attach one bead in the center, while another method is to use spots. For this barrette, I have chosen to use 3 blue spots. When spots like these are used to start the beadwork, it is very important to make sure they are perfectly centered. Failure to do so will result in the beadwork not being symmetrical. I actually measure the diameter of the spot and mark where its points should go through the backing. Because the backing is made with rubber, it can be difficult to push the spot through, so I use a very fine X-Acto® knife blade to delicately slice the backing before placing the spot. Do this very gently, as simply pushing the spot through will almost guarantee that the paper will

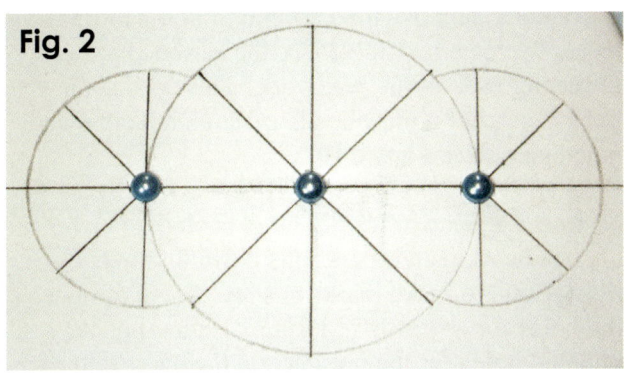

Fig. 2

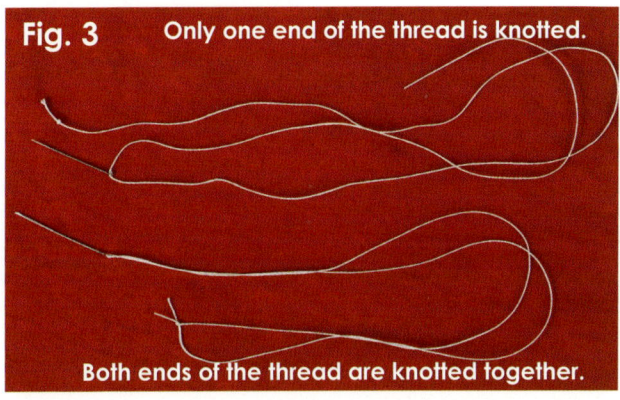

Fig. 3 Only one end of the thread is knotted.

Both ends of the thread are knotted together.

Top: *Single threaded needle (one side of the thread is longer than the other with a knot in the end).*
Bottom: *Double threaded needle (both sides of the thread are the same length and knotted together).*

Thread two sharps beading needles with size D Nymo thread. One needle should have a doubled thread and the other should have a single thread. **See Figure 3.** Start with the double threaded needle and bring it up through the backing exactly ½ bead space away from the center spot. **See Figure 4.**

Fig. 4

Select several beads that are uniform in size and thread them onto this needle. With the single threaded needle, tack down every second bead using the appliqué technique. The grid lines on the template will help you keep the work straight, with the designs lined up properly.

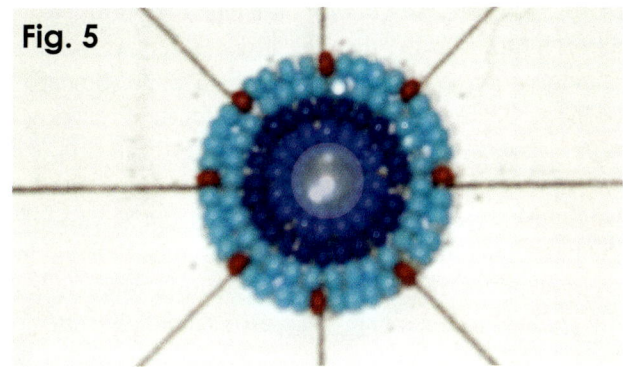

Fig. 5

31

Craftwork Techniques

Fig. 6

Continue the beadwork as described in the medallion chapter, and after completing the center section, you can bead the two side sections. In this barrette, these are a little smaller than the center section and are done in a variation of the same design. However, a different design using the same basic colors could also be used, providing a nice contrast with the center, so be creative!

Assembling The Barrette

Now that the beadwork panel is complete, as shown below in Figure 7, it is time to put the barrette together.

Fig. 7

The first thing to do is decide what type of barrette back you want to use. The metal barrettes used to back these pieces are made in either France or China. The French version consists of two pieces and is a little sturdier than the Chinese version, which is made in three pieces. **See Figure 8 & 9.** They are both satisfactory, and although I prefer the French type, I am using a Chinese made barrette in this example. Be careful to select a size that best fits the beadwork panel, but another consideration is who the barrette is for? If the person has fine hair, using a large barrette back would not be wise. Similarly, if the person has thick hair, the use of a small barrette would not work well.

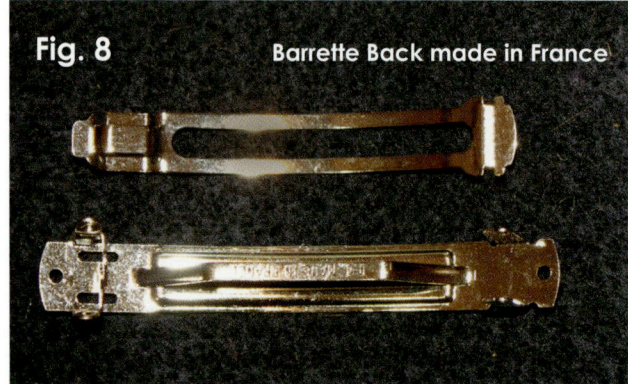

Fig. 8 — Barrette Back made in France

Fig. 9 — Barrette Back made in China

If you are not making a barrette for anyone in particular, I recommend using a medium size so that it will fit most people. Regardless of which hardware you choose, the barrette must be taken apart in order to attach it to the beaded panel and to complete the leather backing.

Once the barrette has been taken apart, you will note that each end has a hole in it. These will be used to attach it to the beadwork panel. Center the barrette on the panel and using a needle that is double threaded with size D Nymo thread, go through the hole and the beadwork panel. Then come back through the beadwork panel on the outside of the hole. Tie the two ends together with a couple of knots and then repeat for the other side. Place the barrette back on the center back of the beadwork. This does not have to be exact, but it must be placed straight across and not angled. **See Figure 10.**

Next, cut a piece of leather large enough to cover the beadwork panel. Press this down on the back of the barrette to make marks to show where to punch the holes for covering it. Using a leather punch, punch 2 holes for the uprights on the hinge end of

32

the barrette and 2 more holes on the clasp end. With a sharp pair of scissors, cut a slot connecting the two holes on the clasp end as shown in **Figure 11**. Make sure that the holes and the slot line up with the two uprights on the clasp.

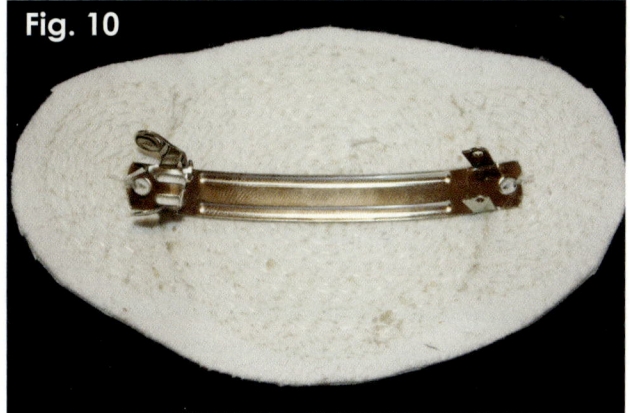

Barrette hardware centered and stitched.

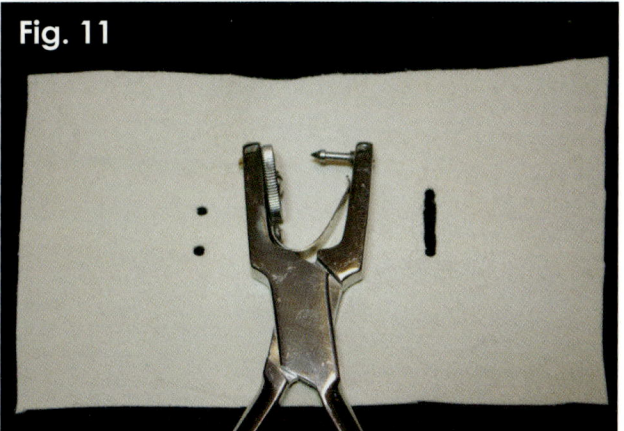

Leather Backing: Punch 4 holes, then on the clasp side only, connect them by cutting the leather to create a slot as shown.

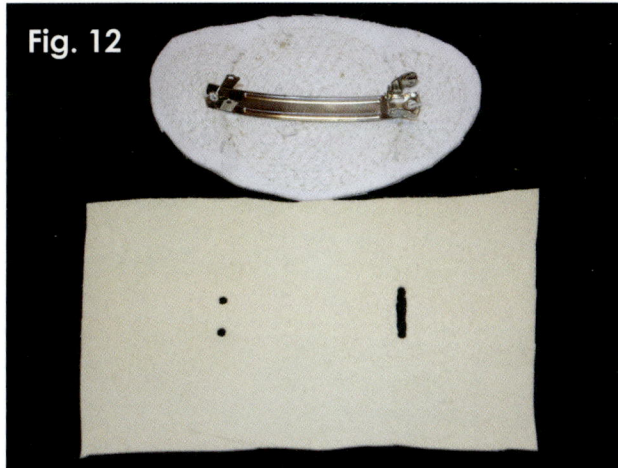

Note that the 2 holes line up with the prongs on the hinge end and the slot lines up with the 2 prongs on the clasp end.

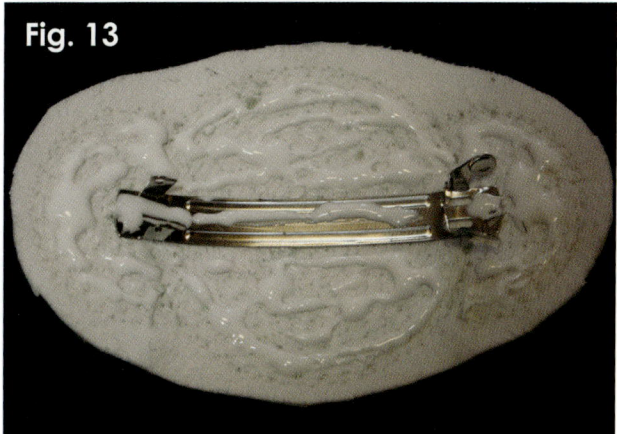

Put some glue on the back of the beadwork and the barrette hardware.

Spread glue over the back surface of the beadwork panel and on the barrette itself, making sure it is thoroughly covered. While the glue is still wet, place the leather over the uprights and the clasp, pressing it firmly onto the entire beadwork panel. Allow this to dry before proceeding. **Figures 12-14**.

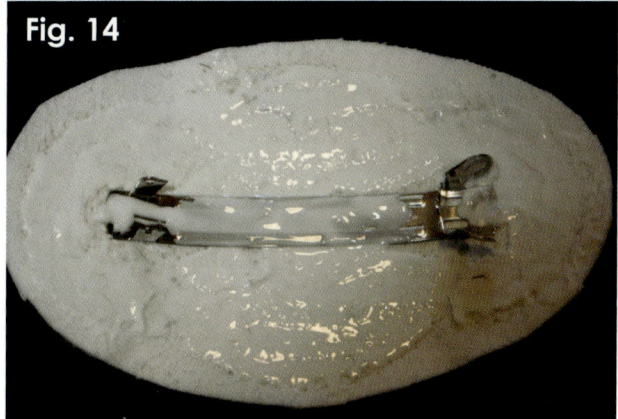

This shows the glue after it is spread over the entire surface, including the barrette back.

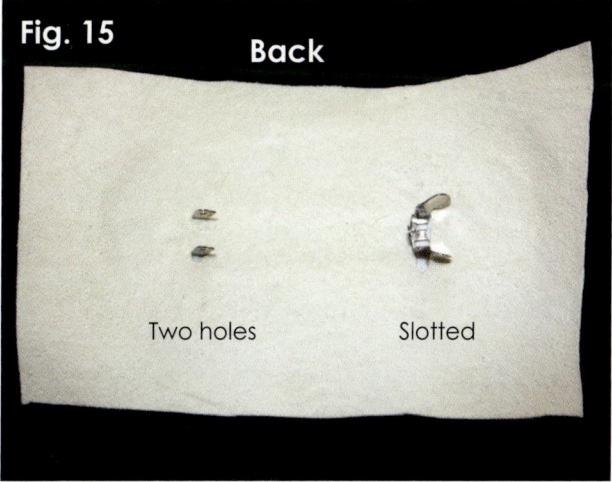

Place the leather backing over the barrette ends.

33

Craftwork Techniques

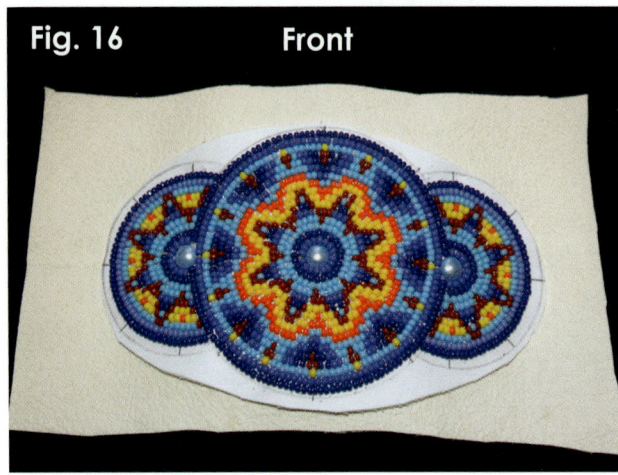

Fig. 16 — Front

Trimming The Backing

When the glue is thoroughly dry, trim the excess leather and backing away from the edge of beadwork, being careful not to cut into any threads.

Fig. 17

Trim the backing close to the beadwork using a pair of sharp scissors.

Fig. 18

To trim the corners, first cut in closely from one side, being very careful not to cut any threads!

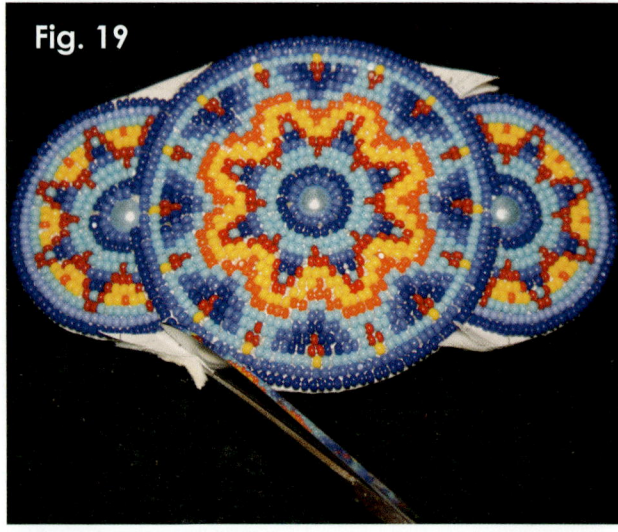

Fig. 19

Then from the opposite side, cut closely into the corner to finish the cut.

Fig. 20

Make sure the tip of scissors gets into the corner, continuing to watch out for any threads.

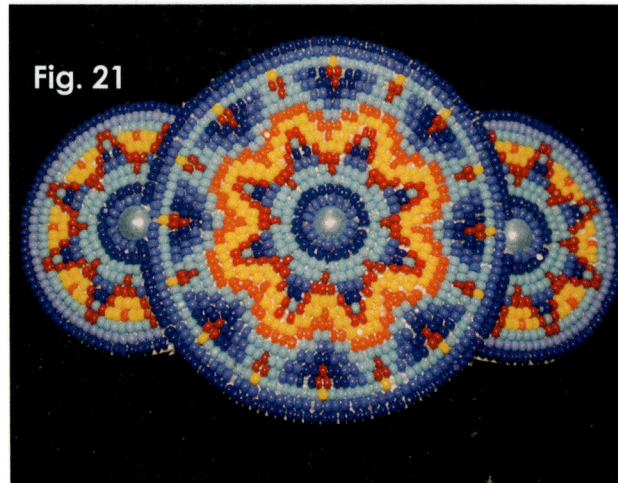

Fig. 21

Finished barrette with excess backing trimmed away.

34

Barrettes

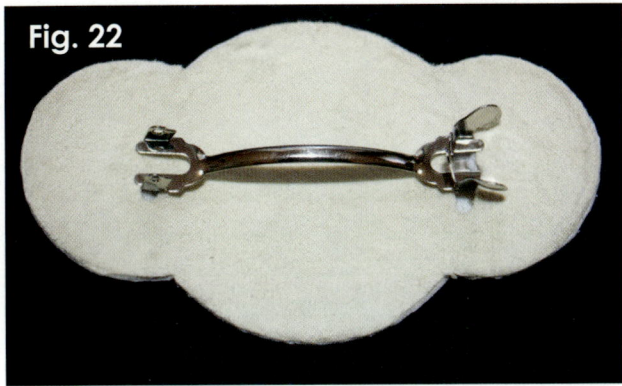

Put the bridge piece back into place.

Reassembling The Barrette Clasp

To put the barrette hardware back together, place one side of the clip into one of the holes of the bracket. Then, ever so gently with your fingers, pull the bracket apart and put the other side of the clip into the other hole. Squeeze the bracket back to its original place, and finally check to make sure the clasp works well.

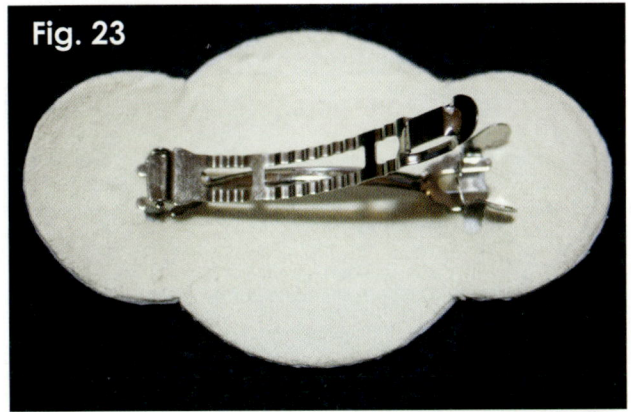

Put the clasp back into the holes of the barrette back.

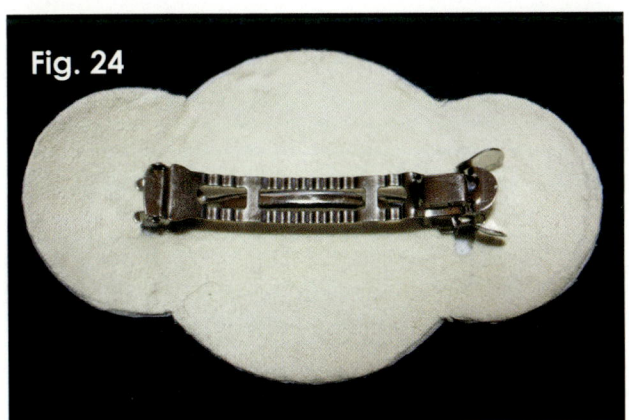

Closed barrette ready for edge beading.

Edge beading

Edge beading provides the finishing touch for the barrette. In this example, a picot edge is created with a base of two beads. Begin by threading a needle with size "D" Nymo thread. Double the thread, then wax it and tie an overhand knot in the end. Insert the needle from the back of the panel, pushing it through the leather and backing, and coming out at the edge of the beadwork. Put 5 beads on the needle and stitch from the back to the front again, about one bead width away from the first stitch. Then come back up through the last two beads. For each successive stitch, put 3 beads on the needle and again, make the same stitch and come back up through the last two beads each time. This will cause 2 beads to be stacked up, with 1 bead left standing on end to form the picot edge. Continue completely around the barrette until you reach the starting point. Then to complete the edging, place 1 bead on the thread and go down through the first two beads and through the backing. Tie off the thread, thus completing the barrette.

Note the spacing of the edge beading at the inside corner.

The close-up view of the edge beading in **Figure 25** clearly shows the wider spacing of the rows where it crosses a tight corner. Do not crowd these stitches!

You have now completed a beautiful piece of beadwork that you can be very proud of!

Chapter Five

Loom Beaded Belts

Materials

This project requires materials to do the actual beaded strip and materials on which to mount the strip and create the belt.

▶ **Bead Loom**

▶ **Thread for warp:** Button thread, heavy Nymo or carpet thread all work well.

▶ **Thread for weft:** Size D Nymo

▶ **Needles:** 10 Beading or 11 Sharps work well.

▶ **Beads:** 8/0, 10/0, 11/0, 12/0 or 13/0 are all acceptable sizes for loomwork.

▶ **Leather for backing:** Latigo, harness leather or split cowhide work well and these can either be dyed or left natural.

▶ **Buckles:** Metal buckles

▶ **Decorative studs:** Different styles can be used and are available in many different sizes, colors and shapes.

Before stringing the loom you must have a design and I strongly suggest drawing this out. Unless you are using a very simple pattern, it is difficult to bead without having the design graphed out in color. Garters, bags, shirt strips, and necklaces are but a few of the clothing pieces that were decorated with loom beadwork. Ideas for beadwork designs can be developed by studying photos in books, auction catalogs, the internet, etc. that show loom beaded items. Belts were not the only beaded items that were decorated using this technique. Also, most museums with a collection of Native American material will have some examples of loom beadwork and many of these are available online.

For sketching a design, you can choose from several commercial bead graph papers that are available. The design I have drawn for the belt in this project is shown below and is 43 beads wide. When drawing designs, it is only necessary to do the portions that are not repeated, thus saving time and effort.

Patterns

There are as many designs for looms in existence as there are pieces of wood! Most looms consist of one

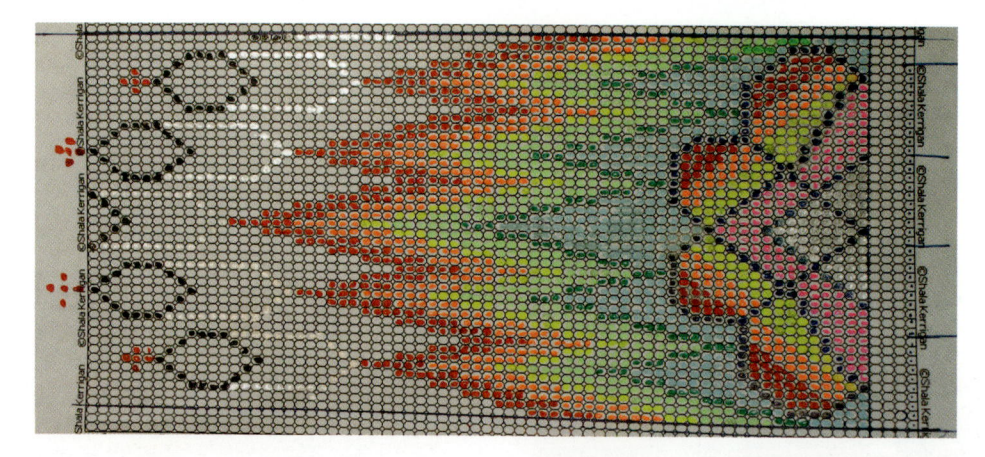

Craftwork Techniques

piece of wood for the base and two pieces of wood for uprights. This particular loom is long enough to bead a 38"- 40" belt. Strung between two nails on each of the wooden uprights is a row of beads which are the same size as those used in my belt. I also put several nails along the side of the upright. These nails reduce the stress on the beads that are used to separate the warp threads when stringing the loom.

Thread a beading needle using size D Nymo. This will be a single thread and used for the weft thread. A long or short needle can be used but keep in mind that a longer needle will allow you to go through more beads at one time, thus making the work go faster. You are now ready to string beads on the weft thread in order to begin the actual beading process. Looking at your graphed design, find the center row. This is the row with which you will begin the beading. Pick the beads for the center row according to your pattern. The next step is to push this first row of strung beads up under the warp threads. Separate the beads so that there is one warp thread between each bead, as shown below. Starting at the side with the needle, begin going back through the beads, making sure that your needle passes over the *top* of the warp threads.

Warp threads are those that are strung long ways on the loom, and strong thread that will not stretch should be used for these. Nymo, carpet thread, or heavy cotton thread can be used, but if using Nymo it should be pre-stretched before stringing. If the warp threads do not stay tight, it makes the beading more difficult. When starting to string the loom, start in the center and work your way out going back and forth until the outer edge is reached. Tie off the thread, being careful to maintain even tension on all the threads. Then start at the center again and work your way out to the other side.

38

Go through as many beads as possible based on the length of the needle you are using. Continue until you are through the whole row and the needle comes out the other side. Pull the thread completely through, gently snugging up the row.

String the second row of beads, continuing to follow the pattern you have drawn. Then, pull the beads down to the end of the thread, pushing them up in between the warp threads as before. At this time, make sure that this second row is pushed snugly against the first row and that both rows are straight across the warp threads. Run your needle back through this row of beads, again making sure your needle and thread are going through the beads on top of the warp threads. Continue adding rows until your thread is too short to complete a row. To tie off the weft thread, go back through 7 to 10 beads and bring your needle out, making sure you are on the underside of the warp threads. Run the weft thread under a warp thread and bring it up so that about half the length of your remaining thread is on either side of the warp thread. Then tie a knot around the warp thread. Once the knot is tied, clip off the loose tails of thread.

Now go back to where you began the first row and thread your needle with the tail of the weft thread that was left there and tie it off in the same method you used when you ran out of thread. Rethread your needle as before and beginning at the opposite side from where you tied off the old thread, tie a knot around one of the warp threads about 7-10 beads in. Then run the needle through these beads and to the outside edge of the work, as shown in the above photo. This puts the thread in position to continue beading. Continue adding rows until you reach the end of your bead strip. Some beadworkers, myself included, find it more comfortable to bead in the same direction when adding rows on either side of the center row, so I just flip the loom around every time I start a new thread.

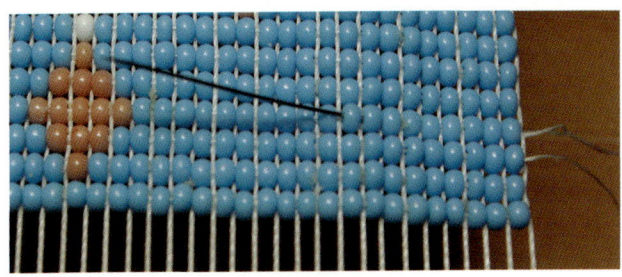

When you finish the last row, end the beadwork by weaving the weft thread back through the last 3 or 4 rows of beads. This will strengthen the end of the beadwork strip, and because you have done this back weaving, you do not have to tie a knot. Just bring the thread up in the middle of the work as shown above and clip it off. Do the other half of the strip the same way and your beaded strip will be completed.

Craftwork Techniques

To take the piece off the loom, wrap some tape around the warp threads, pulling in the sides so that the tape will not show when it is folded under the beadwork. Since the leather backing has been dyed black, I have used black electrical tape to wrap the ends of the beadwork. This color will blend in with the backing and will not be noticeable. With both ends of the finished beadwork taped, proceed to cut the warp threads on each end of the piece.

40

Loom Beaded Belts

The leather for mounting the belt should be cut long enough to fit you and wide enough for a ½" to ¾" border on both sides. Also, if adding decorative studs, make sure you allow enough extra space for these as well. It is important to double check the length of the leather, making sure it will fit around your waist and allow some extra room to grow. Next, cut 4 straps for the buckles that are just wide enough to fit through your buckles, as shown on the facing page. Make two of them 3" long to attach to the buckles and the other two 6" long for the tongues.

One hole is needed ½" in from one end and another hole is needed 1" from the first hole that you punched. See the top photo. A slit is made in the leather by cutting between the holes with an X-Acto® knife.

Punch some small holes with an awl for sewing the buckle in place. Put the strap up through the buckle, over the post, and back down through the other side of the buckle. After lining up the small holes that you punched, stitch the leather strap together using a glovers needle and imitation sinew. These stitches are made by sewing up and down through the pre-punched holes. When you reach the last hole, stitch backwards to the beginning. Tie off the sinew on the back side and carefully melt the ends to secure the knot, preventing it from coming untied.

The straps that go through the buckles should be long enough so there are enough holes to accommodate different waist sizes. It is important to make sure you have some extra length here, as belts are a major project, and as time marches on, your waist size may change. Eventually, this extra length may come in handy. Punch a hole in each strap about 1 ½" from the tip, then place 5-7 holes ½" apart. You don't need to punch holes in the last 2 ½" or so because this is where the straps will be sewn to the belt. With an awl, punch two rows of small holes for this stitching.

Measure the distance on the beaded strip about 2 beads in from each side and 2 rows in from each end.

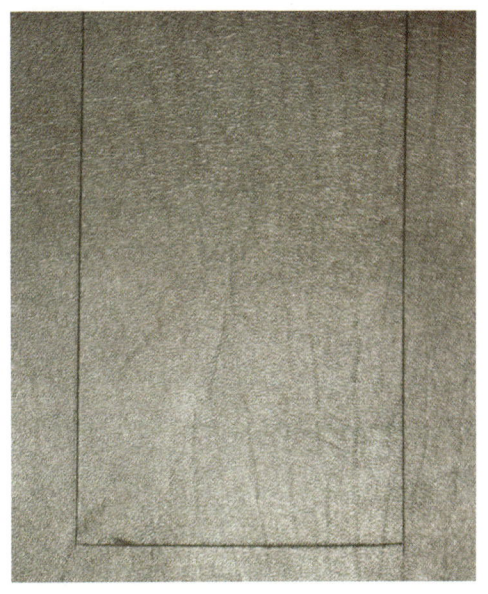

Score the back of the leather with an awl.

41

Craftwork Techniques

This will be a rectangle with dimensions that are just inside the beaded strip all the way around. Turn the leather over and working from the back side, find the center line along its length. Using the tip of an awl, mark this rectangle on the leather by lightly scoring it. This is where the stitches for sewing the bead strip to the belt will be located.

The next step is to actually punch the holes for stitching the beadwork to the leather backing. There are several different methods you can use. I place a heavy duty needle in my sewing machine and set the machine for a long stitch, leaving it un-threaded. Note: If you are using this technique, make sure your sewing machine is sturdy enough to handle leather. Some machines have a clutch system that allows the machine to puncture thick leather. Following the scored line on the back side, run the leather through the machine. This will leave you with pre-punched holes for attaching the bead strip.

Holes made with a sewing machine set for a long stitch.

Another method is to punch holes approximately 1/8" apart with an awl. This requires a great deal more time and effort than punching the holes with a sewing machine, but it works equally well.

When sewing the beadwork to the leather, there is a technique I use to keep the beadwork flat. If you just lay the bead strip flat on the leather and stitch it, the beadwork will be stretched and pulled when the belt is worn. This will weaken the beadwork over time. Conversely, if it is stitched too loosely, it will pucker and will not lay flat. In order to stitch the beadwork to the leather so that it lays flat when worn, simply hold it in a gentle curve while stitching. If you hold it up this way, the weight of the belt itself will be enough to give it the proper gentle curve.

To attach the beadwork to the leather, start the sewing in the center. Thread a regular sewing needle with size D Nymo. Double the thread, wax it and tie a knot in the end. Come up through the center hole of the leather and through the beadwork, three beads in from the outside edge. Then sew back down through the next hole. Come back up through the next hole, and so on until your reach the end of the bead strip. If you run out of thread, tie it off on the back side and start a new one. When the first section is completed, go back to the middle and stitch the other half. Once you have finished one side, repeat this process for the other side. On each end, stitch between the rows as you have done on the sides. I like to add a second row of stitches at each end to give added strength.

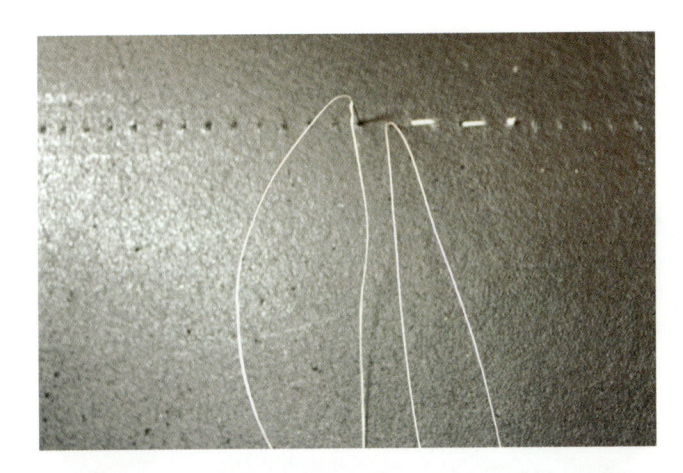

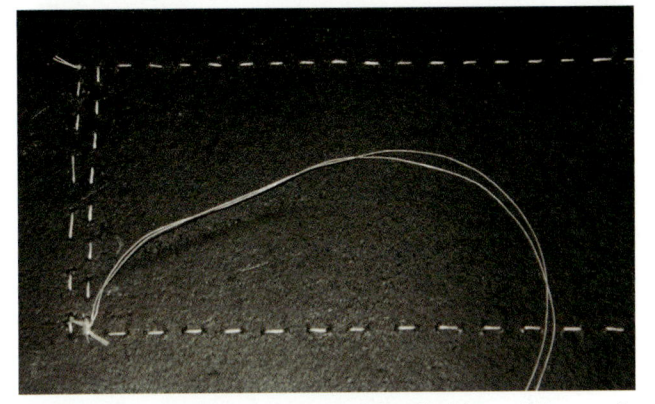

Loom Beaded Belts

Back view of belt showing double stitching at the end.

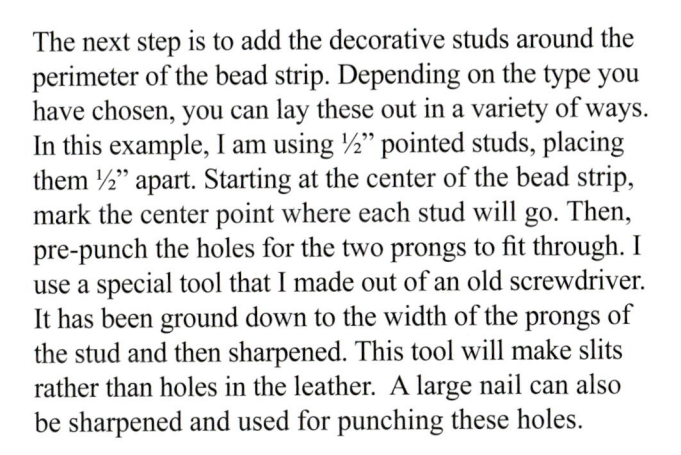

When the belt is laying flat after being mounted on the leather, there will be some pucker to the beadwork. However, when it is worn, it will lay flat and smooth as seen in the photo on the facing page.

The next step is to add the decorative studs around the perimeter of the bead strip. Depending on the type you have chosen, you can lay these out in a variety of ways. In this example, I am using ½" pointed studs, placing them ½" apart. Starting at the center of the bead strip, mark the center point where each stud will go. Then, pre-punch the holes for the two prongs to fit through. I use a special tool that I made out of an old screwdriver. It has been ground down to the width of the prongs of the stud and then sharpened. This tool will make slits rather than holes in the leather. A large nail can also be sharpened and used for punching these holes.

Using a ruler, mark the position where each slit will be, and then using the special tool, push the tip through the leather to cut the slits. It is a good idea to have a piece of wood behind the leather so that only the leather ends up with slits in it! I make several sets of slits at a time and then put in the studs. Continue until all the studs line the edges of the belt. The studs can be placed across the ends as well or these can be left plain, as I have done here.

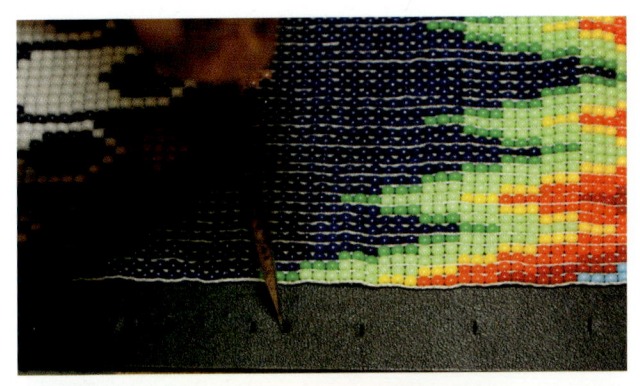

43

Craftwork Techniques

The photo below shows the belt with the studs in place. It is positioned as if it were being worn and you can see that the beadwork is flat against the leather instead of being puckered as it is when laying flat.

Now the buckles and straps need to be attached to the belt. You must decide where to place these, but I like to put them in line with the outer edges of the beaded strip. However, this is not required. Using an awl, pre-punch holes that will line up with holes previously punched in the tongues and buckle straps. Stitch the buckle straps to one side of the belt using a glovers needle and imitation sinew. Sew in one direction then back stitch and tie a knot on the back side of the belt. Then, carefully melt the ends to seal them.

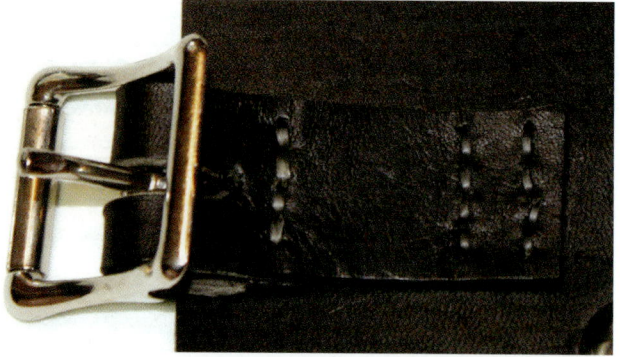

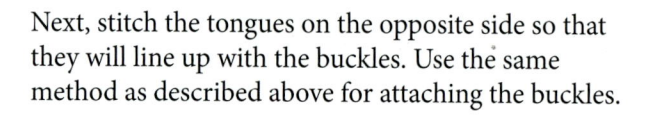

Next, stitch the tongues on the opposite side so that they will line up with the buckles. Use the same method as described above for attaching the buckles.

Loom Beaded Belts

Just a few final touches and the belt will be finished. Use some leather edge dressing, such as Fiebings, on all the exposed edges of the leather. This will give them a shiny, finished look. Some craftsmen cover the back of the belt with black duct tape in order to protect the stitching and cover the folded prongs of the studs, but this is up to you. You now have a completed belt that should last for many years.

45

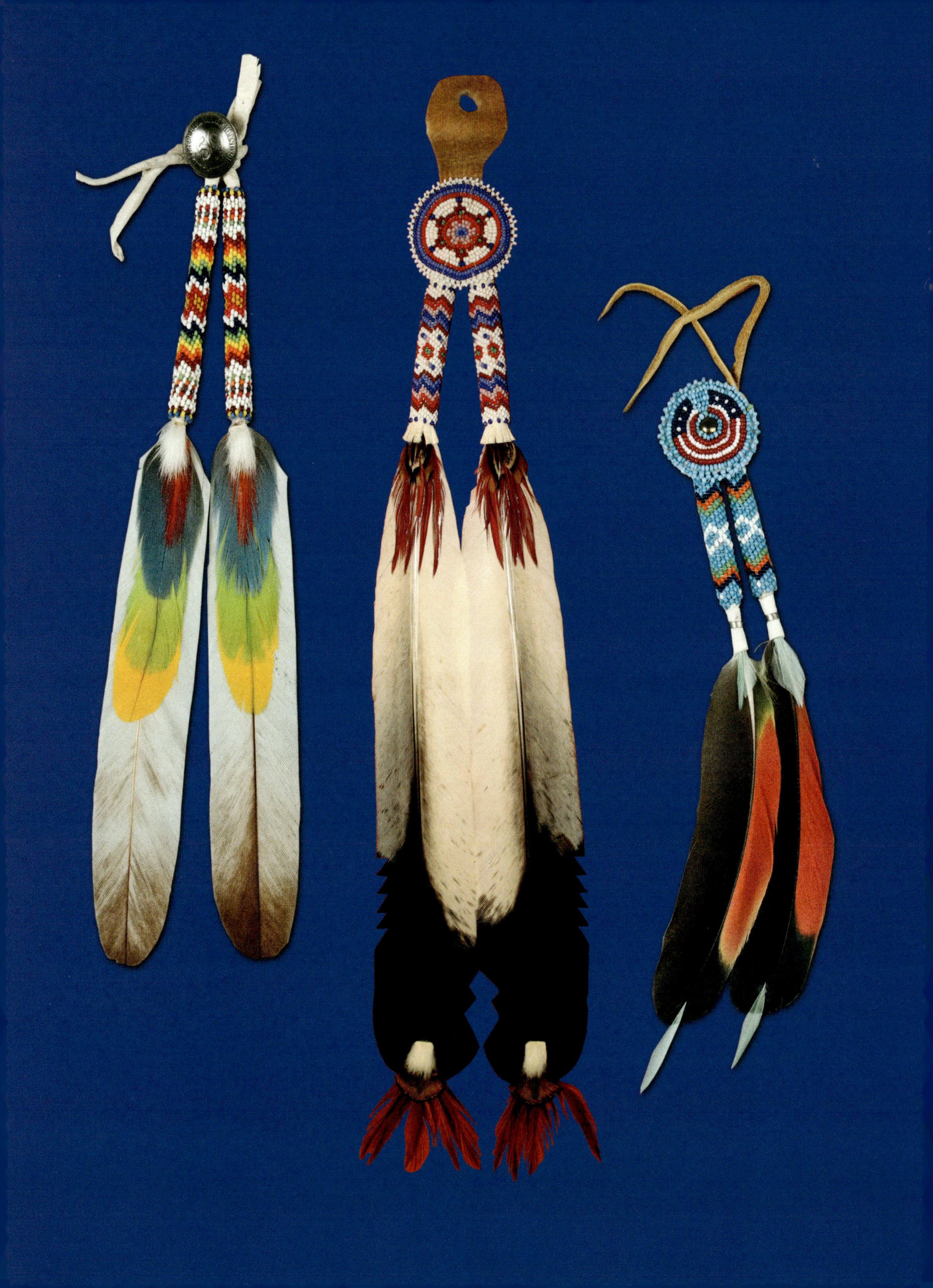

Chapter Six

Scalp Feathers

Scalp feathers are worn by male Straight Dancers and Feather Dancers, and even Traditional Dancers often make use of these ornate feathers that hang from the roach headdress. There are many different styles of scalp feathers, and in this chapter, we will construct a simple pair, along with suggestions for several variations.

Materials

▶ **Large pair of feathers:** Traditionally, these were eagle tail feathers, but now substitutes are used that can be obtained from various Indian trading posts or even on eBay! Pheasant, turkey, and macaw are all used these days to make a set of scalp feathers. Tail feathers work best; however, wing feathers can also be used but these will usually result in a shorter set of feathers. The length is a matter of personal preference as well as the availability of materials, but this can be adjusted using small dowel rods or even toothpicks. The feathers used here are from a hybrid turkey and not perfect, having ragged tips and with one quill longer than the other. However, they have some nice markings and careful trimming will improve them.

▶ **Decorative Feathers:** Many different kinds of feathers can be used to decorate the main feathers, and the ones pictured at the right are dyed goose plumes. Pheasant, grouse, Japanese Chicken, hackle, parrot, macaw and peacock are just some of the small feathers that can also be used for this purpose, and it is simply a matter of taste and personal preference. The key is to use decorative feathers that are not too large and that do not overpower the two larger, main feathers.

▶ **Thread:** Used for wrapping the quills. I like to use German thread as it usually seems to be a little stronger and is available in a wider range of colors.

▶ **Scissors:** Sharp scissors are a must here and I like the Gingher brand. The ones shown in the photo are the smaller embroidery or craft type and are very sharp. I keep one pair of these separate from my other scissors, and I use them exclusively for trimming feathers.

▶ **Medallion:** See the chapter on medallion making for this. Other items that can be used are an abalone shell disc, German Silver conchos, etc; however, I prefer a beaded medallion as it will go well with the beaded feather sockets.

Trimming The Feathers

The first step in completing this project is to trim the large feathers into the shape that you want them.

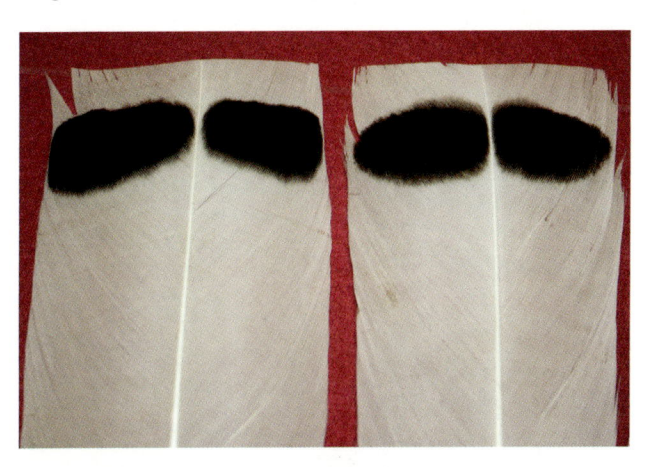

Trim the ragged tips off the feathers using the sharp scissors. This cut is made straight across the top.

Craftwork Techniques

Using the scissors, round the tops of the feathers into a gentle curve as shown in the photo at left.

Cut each of the main feathers the same length and strip away the bottom webbing of the feather so you have about 1½" to 2" of bare quill. To do this, grasp the webbing of the feather and pull down toward the bottom of the feather. They should now be identical in length and remaining amount of webbing, as in the photo below.

Very carefully trim the sides of each feather so that the total width is about 1½", making each side of the quill about ¾" wide. Always cut from the tip of the feather down towards the bottom of the quill, as this helps you maintain a straight line. You don't get any do-overs here, so take your time and make the first cut count. When trimming, some craftsmen like to put masking tape on the back of the feather to hold the webbing in place, but I prefer not to. If you do use tape, remove it soon after you finish the cut so that it doesn't leave any residue.

Scalp Feathers

Trim the tips of the feathers again so that they have a nice curve that blends in with the edges of the feather.

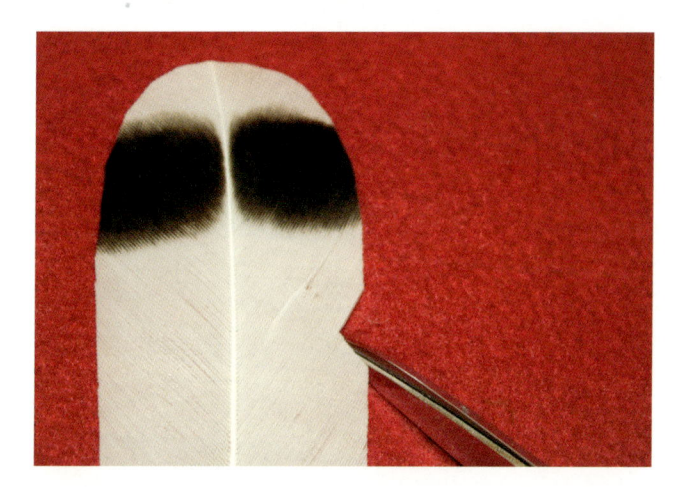

Trim the insides to match the outsides.

Follow the veins of the feather from the bottom of your last notch down to the point where they meet the quill. Cut straight in to the quill at that point, as shown below. Cut in from the other side to match the cut on the opposite side. You may need to do some extra cutting to make the sides perfectly even. This is often necessary because the veins on either side of the feather are usually at different angles.

Next, we will add some decorative cuts. If you cut the webbing upward against the veins at a 90 degree angle, the cut will end in a "V" notch.

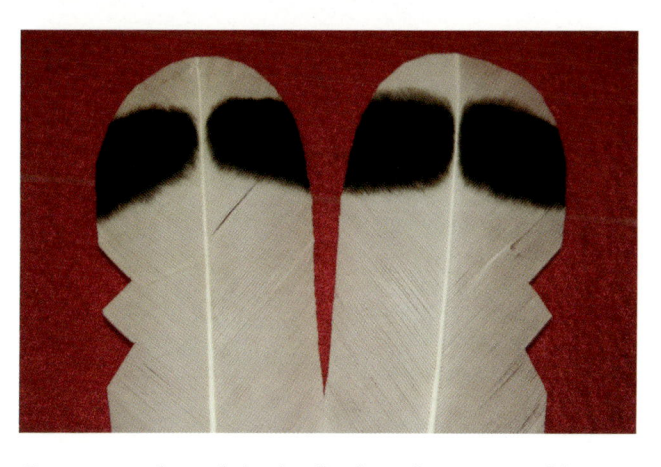

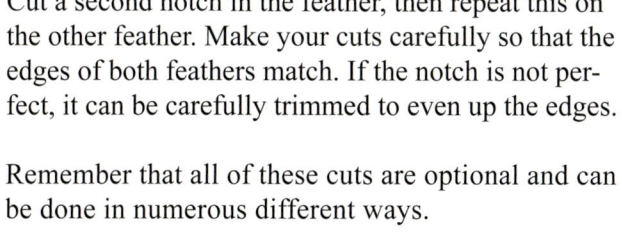

Cut a second notch in the feather, then repeat this on the other feather. Make your cuts carefully so that the edges of both feathers match. If the notch is not perfect, it can be carefully trimmed to even up the edges.

Remember that all of these cuts are optional and can be done in numerous different ways.

49

Craftwork Techniques

Next, I created a bare space of about ½" on the quill in order to do some thread wrapping. So, another straight cut was made ½" lower than the previous one. Then the feather was cut away from the quill. **Note: DO NOT PULL THE FEATHER FROM THE QUILL HERE!** Pulling the feather away from the quill will weaken the feather and may cause the stripping to extend further than you want. Clipping the feather close to the quill works well, leaving the quill intact and the short, remaining stubble will be covered with the thread wrapping. Next, round off these center sections of the feathers using your sharp scissors.

Decorating The Feathers

The next step is decorating the feathers. The colors of the decorative feathers often match colors in the dancer's clothes. Almost any color combination can be used; however, it is important that the colors chosen contrast enough so that they are easily seen on the two main feathers. For this set of feathers, I decided to use dark green, light green and dark blue. I have also used matching colors in the beaded medallion that goes with them.

You can decorate in any order, but in this case I have started with the thread wrapping in the center. Then, I will proceed to the tips and, finally, to the base.

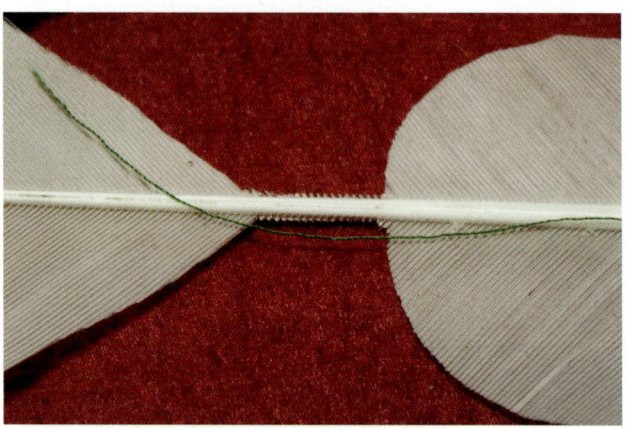

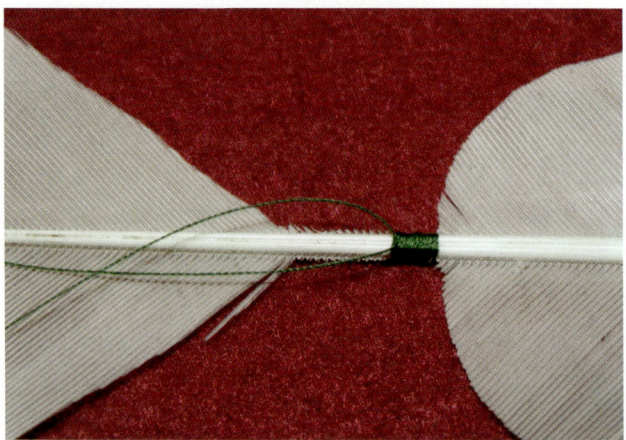

Thread wrapping is a delicate process and takes a little time to master. Your goal is to have the knots on the back side of the quill. Lay one end of the thread down along the quill from the tip of the feather towards the base, as shown above. Begin wrapping at the top of the rounded part of the feather by pinching the thread with one hand at the back of the quill and wrapping with the other. Continue until

50

about 1/3 of the area is covered. Place each wrap of the thread directly next to the previous one. Try to avoid overlapping the thread, as this causes a bulky appearance that does not look smooth and "clean".

After wrapping 1/3 of the area, tie off the thread on the back side of the quill using an adaptation of a square knot. With one end in your right hand and one in the left, place the right hand thread over the left hand thread and through the loop. Then run it through the loop again and pull it down tight. Then place the left hand thread over the right hand thread and through the loop, snugging this down. Do the right over the left one more time, and that will complete the knot. Then, clip off the ends of the thread. Wrap both feathers with the first color thread before moving to the next color. That way, you will keep the same distance and tension on the thread. Proceed wrapping the second and third colors the same way. If you find it necesary, you can put a tiny dab of glue on each knot and let it dry after you are finished.

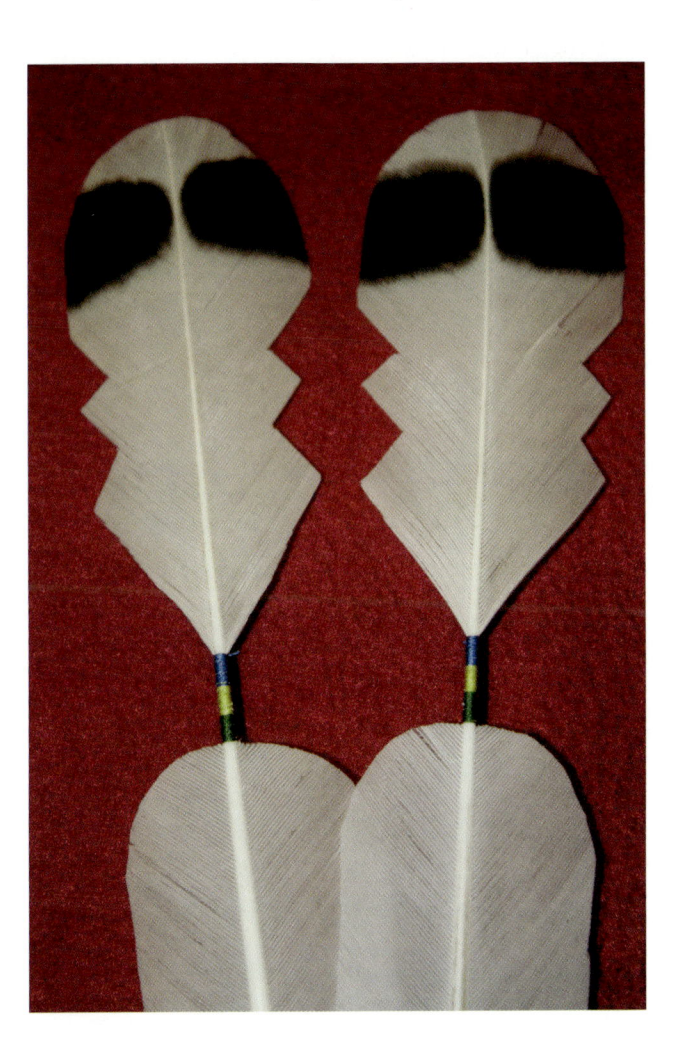

There are many ways to cut the decorative feathers and you can experiment with different cuts to see what you like. For this pair of scalp feathers, I used three different cutting techniques. In order to make these cuts, you will need to pick out a few good feathers. Straighten the goose plumes by using your thumb nail and pressing it against the front of the quill in several spots, moving up the quill. Once the feather is straightened, use your scissors to cut straight across the top of the feather. After cutting the top, decide on the length the feather needs to be and then carefully snip the quill.

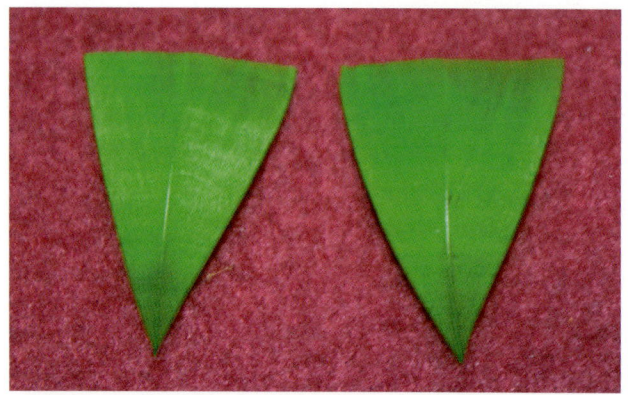

Craftwork Techniques

Dark green feathers trimmed for the first layer of tip decoration.

Light green feathers cut for the second layer of tip decoration.

The next layer of feathers is cut slightly differently. Straighten the feather and clip the top off flat. Next, make two diagonal cuts from the tip of the feather towards the bottom outside of the feather. Before making these cuts, you must decide how wide you want the feather to be. Then clip the feathers to the length you would like.

Glue the first layer of feathers with a small dab of Tacky Glue. Then line up the second layer of feathers (the light green ones) and glue them. The dark blue feathers are cut the same as the first dark green ones, just smaller. Glue the dark blue feathers in place. All three of these feathers are then covered with a small triangle of thin leather that will hide the glue.

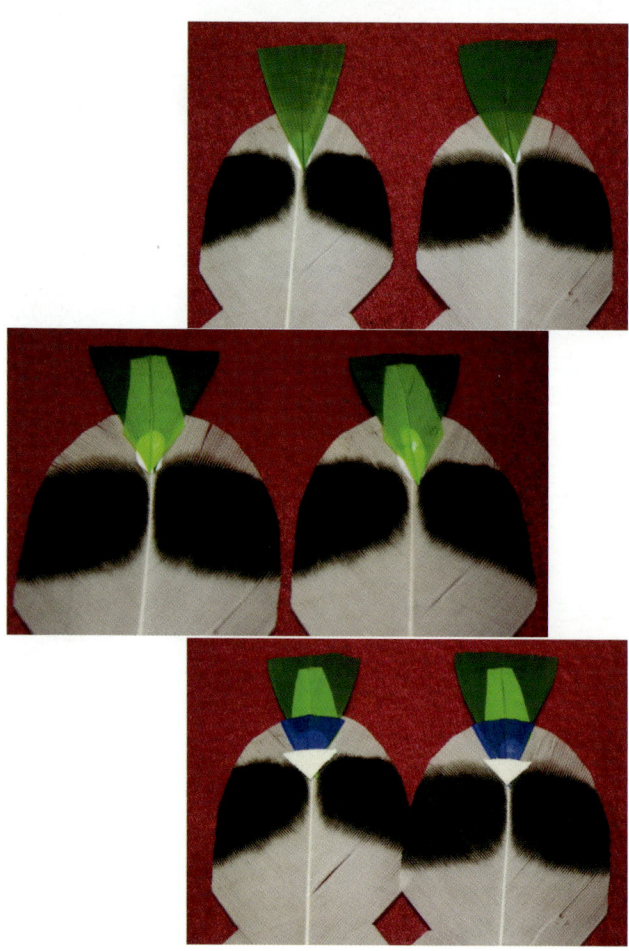

52

Scalp Feathers

The bases of the feathers are decorated in a similar fashion using the same three colors. The feathers for the first layer (dark green) are cut in a half moon shape. Make sure you clip this feather long enough so that the width of the plume covers the width of the feather. The feathers for the second layer (light green) are cut straight across. The feathers for the third layer (dark blue) are cut in the shape of the light green tip feathers except that the angle is a little steeper and the length is longer. See the photos below.

Set the feathers aside and allow the glue to dry thoroughly before proceeding to the next step.

Leather Tabs

Using thin white leather, cut two pieces that are long enough to cover the bottom of each quill, plus about 3 or 4 inches of extra length. Make sure that each piece is wide enough to go completely around a quill.

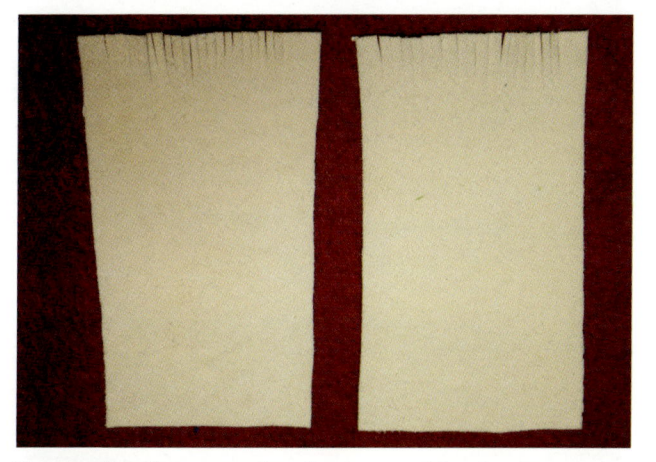

Thin leather for wrapping the base of the feathers. Each piece is fringed at one end, 1/2" in length.

Spread glue from just above the fringe to tip of quill.

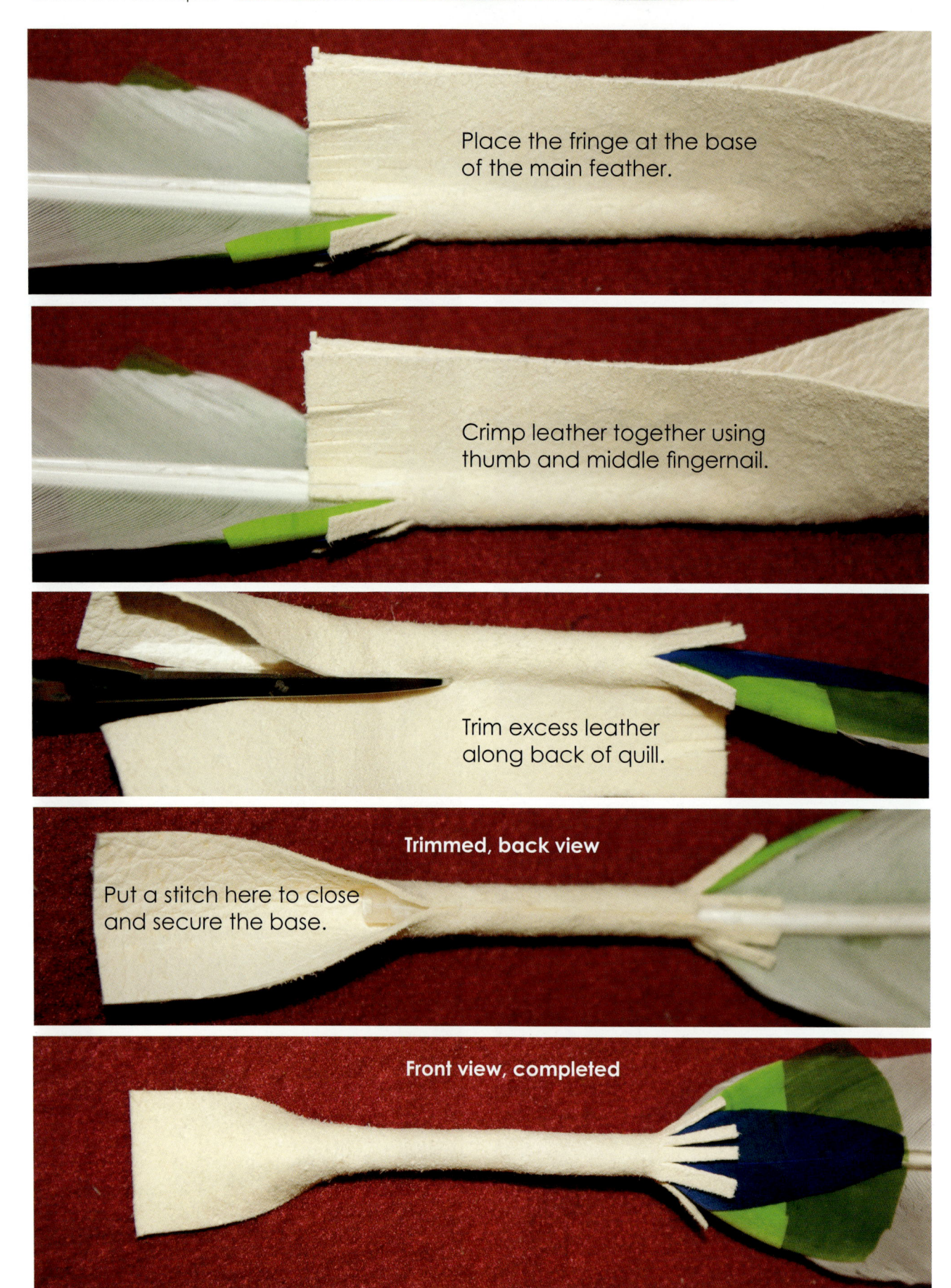

Craftwork Techniques

Place the fringe at the base of the main feather.

Crimp leather together using thumb and middle fingernail.

Trim excess leather along back of quill.

Trimmed, back view

Put a stitch here to close and secure the base.

Front view, completed

Peyote Beadwork

The next step is to add peyote beadwork to cover the base of the quills. Complete, illustrated instructions on this technique can be found in **"Beadwork Techniques of the Native Americans"**, as well as in other books on the subject. Therefore, only a brief description is included here.

Thread a size 11 or 12 "sharps" needle with size A, B or D Nymo thread, depending on the size bead you are going to use. For this project I used 11/0 cut charlotte beads and size D Nymo.

Find the center of the project and begin beading by stitching through the leather at the point where the seam comes together at the back of the quill. String enough beads to go around the quill one time and then count the beads. In this case, it is 17 beads, but this number has to be divisible by 3. Since 3 does not go into 17 evenly, we must round up to 18.
DO NOT DECREASE THE NUMBER OF BEADS; ALWAYS ROUND UP!

Take 1/3 of the beads off leaving 2/3 (12 beads) on the string. Run your needle through the first bead again, and at this point, the thread will be loose. However, it is important to keep it as taut as possible as you proceed. Place one bead of a different color on the needle, skip a bead and draw the needle through the next bead. These first 3 beads should now form a "unit" of 3 beads that are in a stairstep formation. String a second bead on the needle, skip a bead and go through the next bead. This stairstep unit (sometimes called "3-drop") will take on a more uniform configuration with each stitch. Keep adding beads in this way until you complete the first row. When the 6th bead is sewn in place, go through the last bead of the first row, and back through the first bead of this row as well.

The thread will now be in place to begin the next row. At this point, use your fingernail to push the beads around so that they are evenly spaced around the feather. Once the beads are arranged, you must pull the thread snuggly, and each completed row will tighten the work even more. Each subsequent pass around the quill requires 6 beads, with each one being placed directly above the lowest bead in the previous row. A full row consists of 18 beads, requiring 3 passes to complete, with 6 beads added per pass around the quill. That's the technique, and now comes the tricky part, the design!

With only 18 beads to a row, we are very limited on the designs we can use. A zig-zag design of 6 beads can be done, but this will produce only 3 patterns around the quill, which are difficult to see on an object this small. The other option is to use designs consisting of 3 bead units, which allows you to place 6 patterns around the quill. These smaller designs can be seen in their entirety rather than wrapping 1/3 of the way around, and by using contrasting colors, they will be easier to distinguish.

Ready for Peyote Beadwork

Craftwork Techniques

It is also important to use some of the same colors in the beadwork that you have used for the decorative feathers. This helps to bring everything together, making all of the different elements of the scalp feather set flow into a complete and cohesive piece.

For the beadwork design to match this set of feathers, I started in the center, beginning with a first row of off-white beads. The next pass around was the addition of 6 beads, all dark green. Next was 2 passes adding more off-white beads, then 1 pass of medium green, 2 passes of off-white, then 1 of light green, and finally, 2 passes adding off-white beads.

The pattern then changes to 3 passes of dark blue, 2 of off-white, 1 of dark blue, 2 of light green, 1 of dark blue, 2 of medium green, and ending in 3 consecutive passes of dark blue. To cap off the end, one pass of off-white was used. Once the end is reached, go through the last row again and weave the thread back up into the beadwork and clip it off. You do not need to use a knot here as this extra weaving will leave the beads securely in place.

Now, turn the feather around and repeat this process, beading in the other direction toward the end of the leather. To begin, knot the thread and go through the leather backing at the back of the feather as you did when starting. Come up through one of the beads and you are ready to start beading again. Start with dark green beads, first making one pass around, adding 6 beads. The rest of the beadwork will be exactly the same as before! Once completed, repeat the entire process for the second feather. It is very important to make sure you begin beading at exactly the same starting point so that the beadwork matches and is evenly placed. The photo at left shows the completed beadwork.

Attach The Medallion

The next step is to attach a beaded medallion to the feathers. This is done by sewing the leather tabs to the back side of the medallion. Line the feathers up to see where they should be attached. There is some personal taste here as to how far apart you space the

First tab tied at two points in order to keep the feather hanging straight.

56

Scalp Feathers

feathers, and I prefer to place them close together, as shown below. Two stitches are required to hold each feather. A single stitch will allow the feather to rotate, and you want it to stay flat and not rotate.

Both tabs tied in place and with the ends trimmed off.

The photograph at the right shows the finished set of scalp feathers. Notice how the medallion, beaded sockets, and decorative feathers all flow together, giving the entire piece a neatly trimmed look. Yet, these scalp feathers are very simple, with the point being that you do not have to do extremely difficult or complex work to create something that is really nice!

There are several methods that can be used to attach the scalp feathers to your roach and here are some suggestions:

1. Sew a leather thong to the top of the medallion and use this to tie it to the roach string.

2. For attaching the roach with a braid of hair and pinning it through the braid, make a leather "tab" approximately 3/4" wide by 2" long. Cut a hole in the end of the tab that is large enough for your braid to pass through and sew it to the back of the medallion.

3. Sew a piece thin rubber to the back of the medallion where it will not be seen. Make a very small hole in it, and when you slide the roach string through it, the rubber will hold it snugly in place.

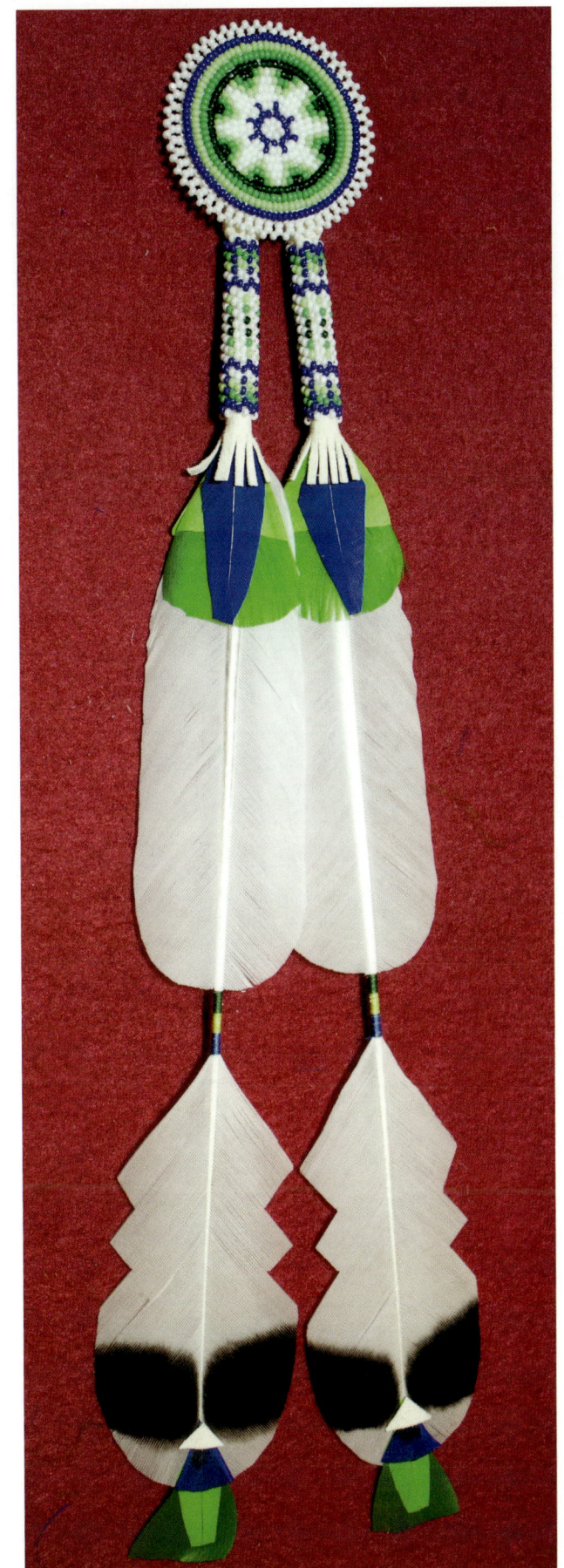

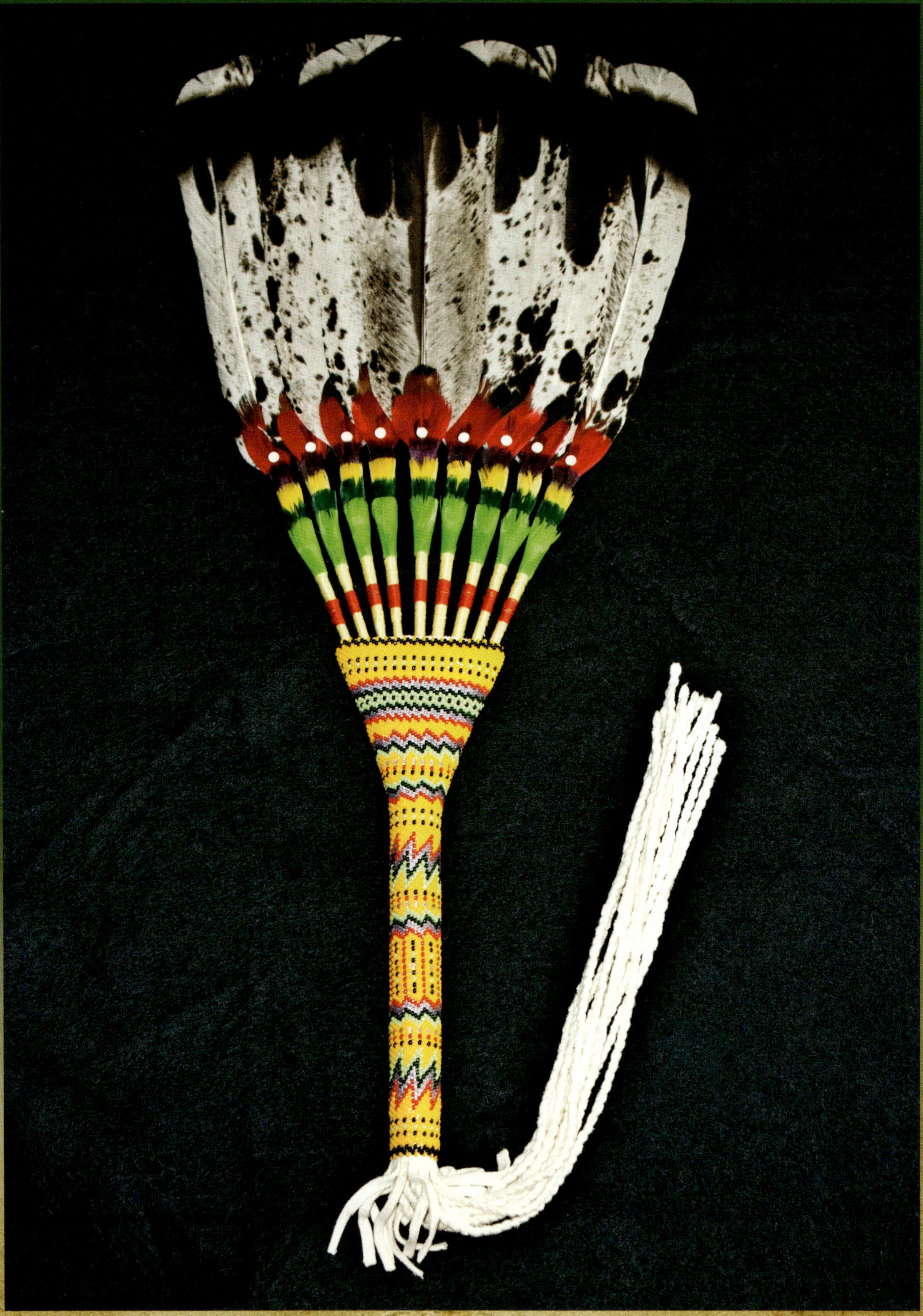

Chapter Seven

Flat Fans

Materials

▶ **Main Feathers:** Turkey tails or wings, macaw tails or wings, as well as feathers from other types of birds can be used for fan making. Many of the Indian trading posts carry these feathers and it is always best to examine the feathers personally so that you can lay them out to see what they will look like when set.

▶ **Decorative Feathers:** Many types of small decorative feathers are normally used to decorate the front and back of the fan at the base of the main feathers, and tip feathers can also be added for a woman's fan. Trim feathers typically come from many different varieties of birds, including various species of macaw, parrot, and pheasant, as well as hackles, goose plumes and various others.

▶ **Wood Dowel:** This is used to form the handle and the size can vary depending on the size of the feathers as well as the size of hand that will carry the fan. Common sizes are 1/2" to 3/4" in diameter, but keep in mind that the addition of the leather covering and the beadwork will make the finished handle larger.

▶ **Body Filler:** An auto body filler product such as Bondo® works well.

▶ **Additional Tools:** Sharp pocket knife for whittling, coarse wood file or rasp for shaping the Bondo®, wax paper and a plastic knife.

▶ **Leather for Covering the Handle:** Thin leather in 1 - 3 ounce weight.

▶ **Twisted Fringe:** Very thin white leather, such as light weight buckskin, is normally used to roll fringe.

A flat fan is a beautiful addition to any set of dance clothes and there are several different styles and techniques fo making one. Some fans are very elaborate and, depending on the type and number of feathers, trim work, beadwork, etc., cost hundreds of dollars. This chapter provides details on a method of constructing a basic fan, and by expanding on these basic techniques, more elaborates styles can be made. In addition, certain details make a fan more suited to being either a man's or woman's fan and these differences are covered as well.

Feather Preparation

It is advantageous to begin a fan by preparing the main feathers first. This will allow you to see how the feathers will "lay out" in the finished fan before they are set into the handle, and it will also help you determine what size handle will look best. For example, the handle should not be big and bulky if the feathers are slim and trim, or shorter types. Conversely, a large fan should have a proportionally larger handle.

Different types of feathers require different handling. For example, Macaw feathers are long and slender and require very little trimming except in length. If you use turkey feathers that are wider than feathers that were traditionally used in fans, they should be trimmed appropriately along the edges so as to make them appear more like real eagle feathers.

Craftwork Techniques

Fig. 6

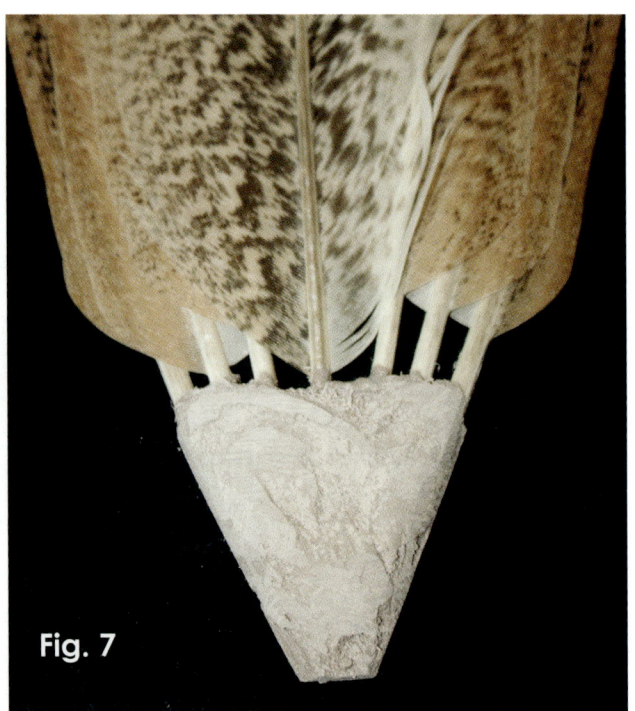

Fig. 7

After trimming off the hardened, excess Bondo® with a sharp whittling knife, it can be smoothed using the coarse file or rasp as shown in the above photo.

Attaching The Handle

The next step is to add the wooden dowel handle, and for this fan, I am using one that is 1/2" in diameter and approximately 7" long. As shown in **Figure 9**, cut one end of the dowel in order to form a flat, stable area on which to mount the base of the feathers. Next, carve the other end of the dowel to form a peg for attaching the fringe. See **Figures 8 & 9**.

Fig. 8

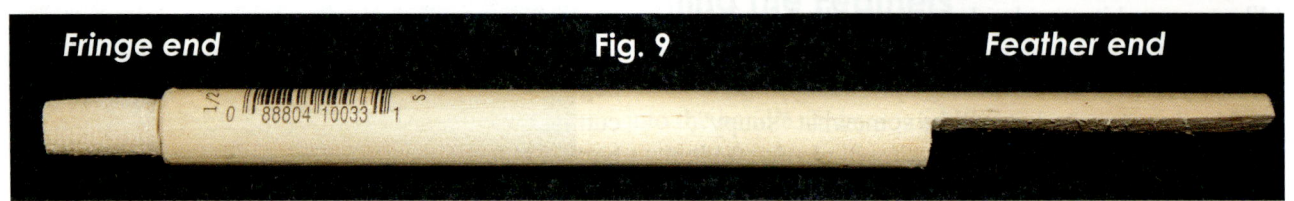

Figure 6 shows how the feathers should look before trimming the Bondo®. Notice that the black band across the top of the feathers creates a gentle arc, with the tips flowing along the same arc. This is one of the characteristics of a well-made flat fan. So again, make sure the feathers are arranged properly before applying the Bondo®, because once it begins to harden, you are committed!

Fringe end   **Fig. 9**   *Feather end*

62

To attach the handle, place the feathers face down on a work surface that is covered with wax paper. After centering the dowel with the flat side down on the base of the feathers, use contact cement to secure the handle to the base. Then spread an even coat of Bondo® over this, covering the dowel and blending it smoothly into the back of the base. Allow this to set for several minutes, then begin shaping the handle.

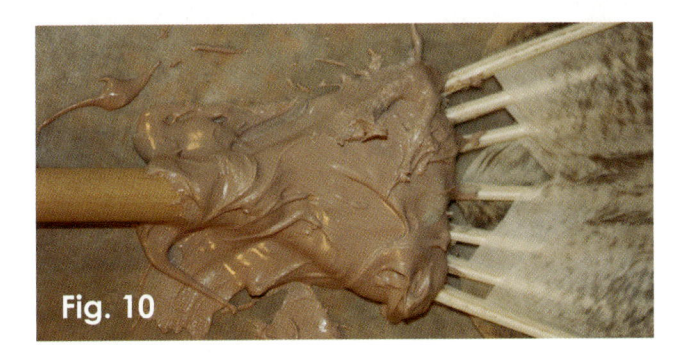

Fig. 10

Shaping The Handle

The goal in shaping the handle is to trim it down so that it is no thicker than the 1/2" dowel and tapers into the natural slope of the feathers. Begin by using the whittling knife to take off the rougher parts and then use the coarse file to remove more of the Bondo®, continuing to refine the shape.

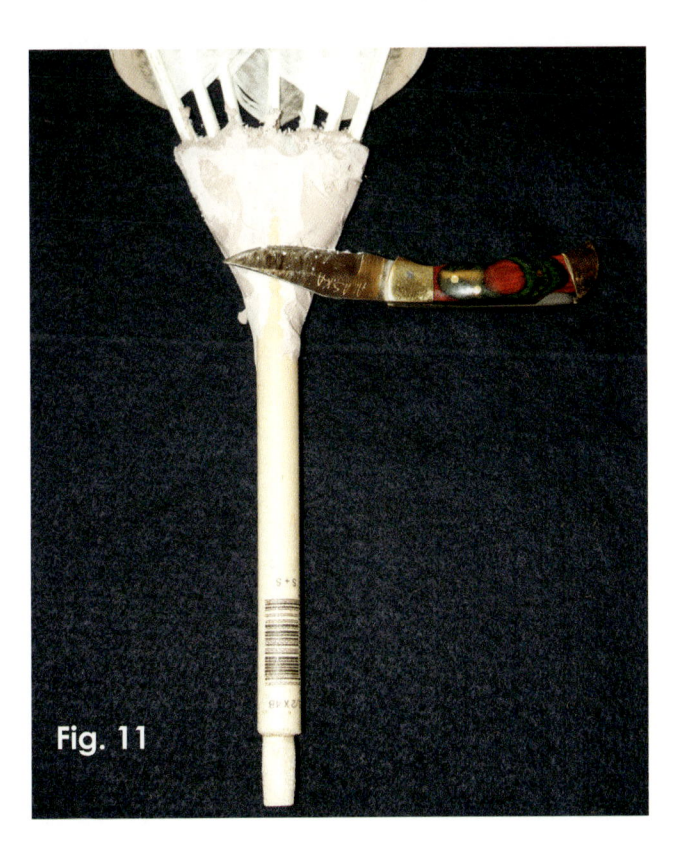

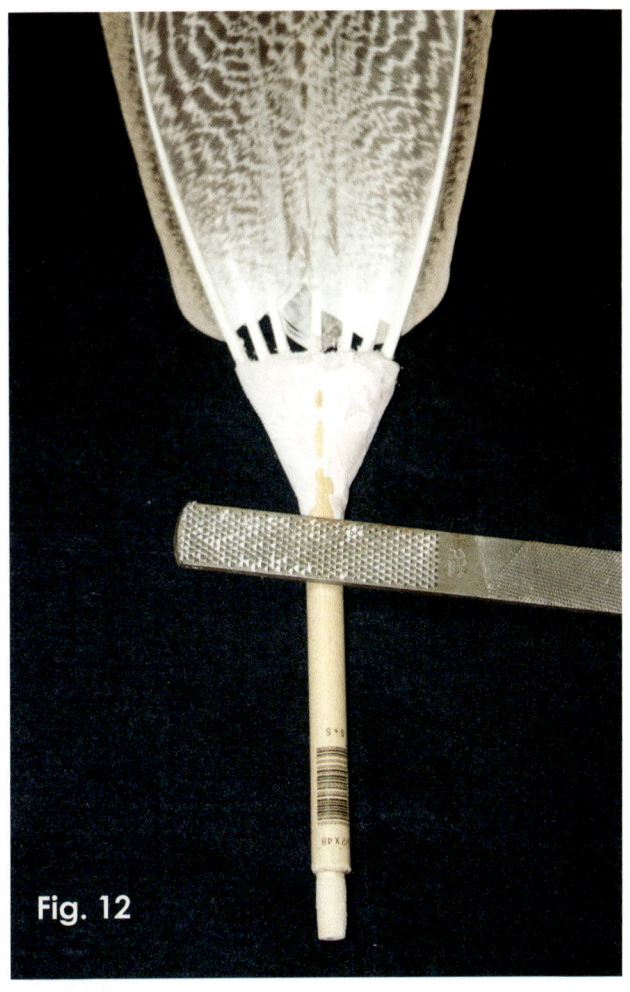

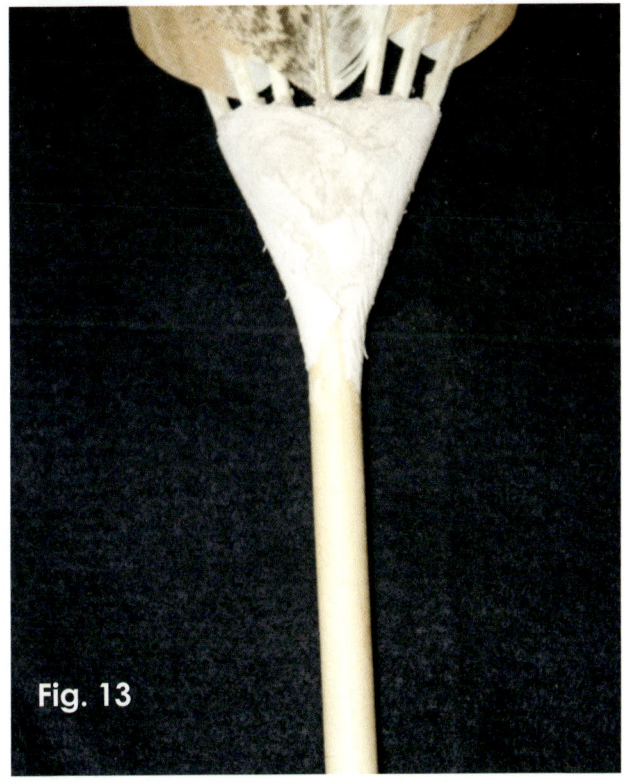

Fig. 12

Fig. 11

Fig. 13

Flat Fans

63

Craftwork Techniques

Repeat the process adding more Bondo®, letting it harden and then trimming and filing it to shape. Continue until you have a nicely shaped handle as shown in **Figures 15 & 16**. The final step is to sand the handle to a smooth finish, first using medium and then fine sandpaper.

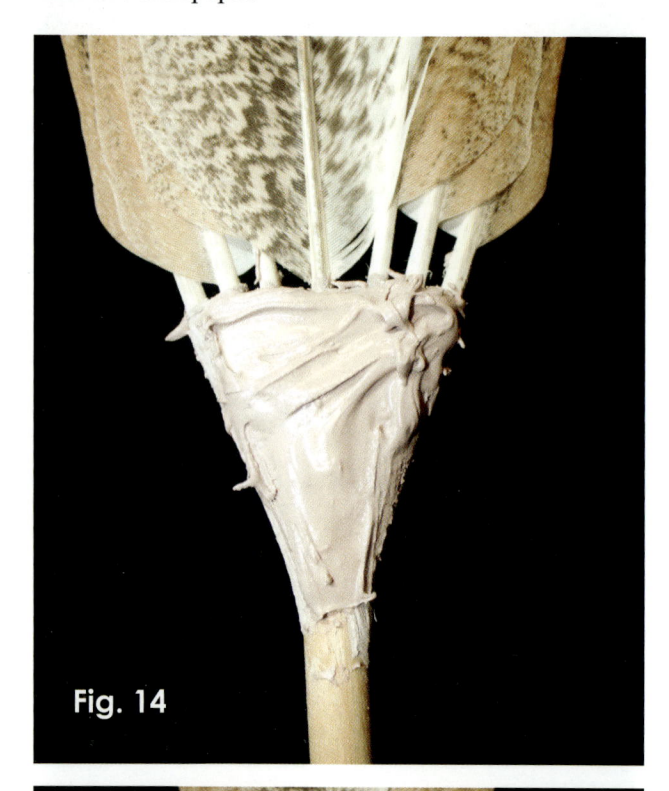

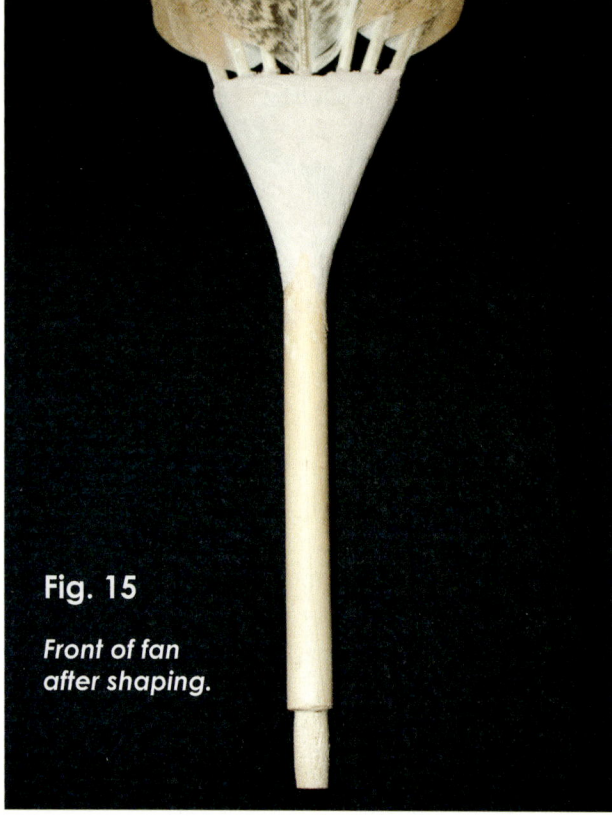

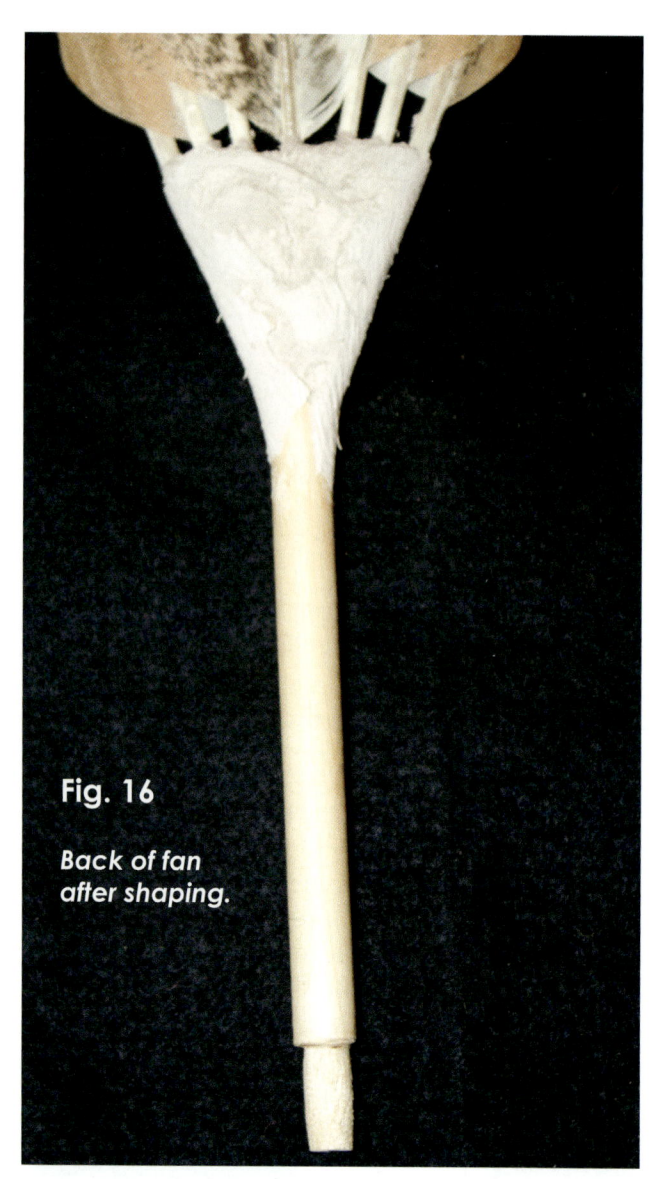

Fig. 14

Fig. 15
Front of fan after shaping.

Fig. 16
Back of fan after shaping.

Adding Decorating Feathers

A very important factor in adding trim feathers is the choice and placement of colors. This requires careful planning and some experimentation, choosing complementary colors, as well as types of feathers that look nice together and enhance the appearance of the main feathers. On some fans, these decorations are very elaborate and for some styles, a more advanced craftsman might decorate each individual feather before it is set. There is another technique that calls for the use of small paper cones and elaborate cutting and trimming of small goose feathers. As the fan constructed here is a simple one decorated only with several layers of dyed goose feathers, the more advanced techniques are not being covered.

After deciding on colors and placement, each trim feather must be straightened and trimmed before gluing it in place. I have chosen to use five bands of color, starting 3" up from the base of the fan. Layer one is yellow, with each of 7 goose feathers cut straight across the top. The quill is then cut off 1½" down from the tip. The two outer feathers will need a little extra trimming so that they do not hang over the edge of the larger turkey feathers. Use Aleene's Tacky Glue® to attach these feathers to the fan. It will dry clear, but it takes more than just a tiny dab at the end to hold them securely in place.

Fig. 18

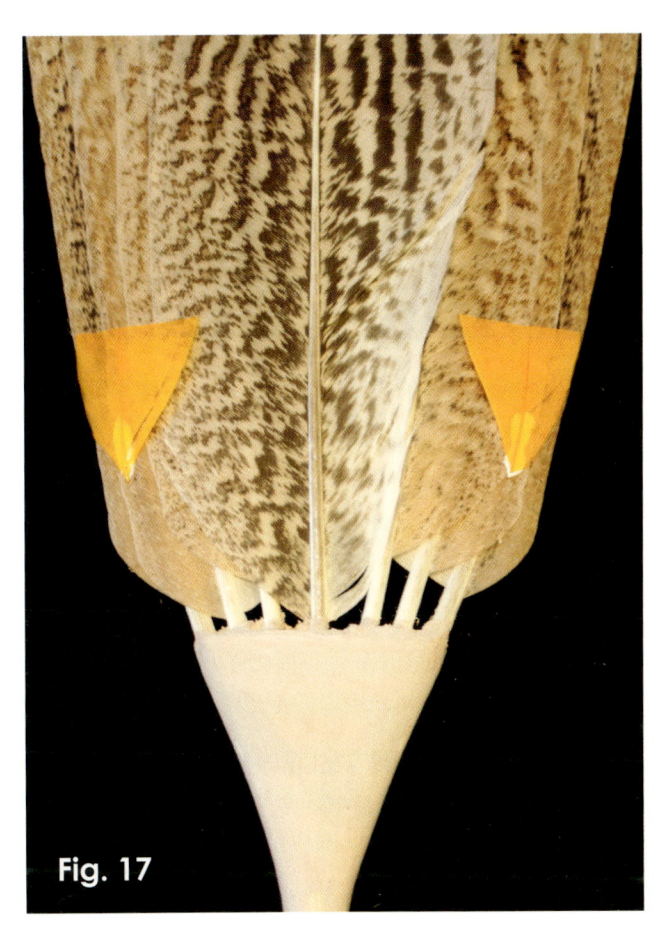

The second row of feathers is maroon in color so as to contrast with the golden yellow of the first row. They are cut in the same way as the first row, again trimming the two outside feathers further, as before. Glue these down starting from the outside and working in toward the center. This row is started ½" below the yellow row.

Fig. 17

Note that the outsides of the feathers are trimmed to not hang over the edge.

Continue gluing the yellow feathers evenly across the fan. The quills of these decorative feathers do not necessarily line up with the quills of the turkey feathers, but rather have their webbing evenly spaced. Note that the 3rd feather from the left lies farther to the right in order to space the "fan" part of the feather correctly, as this is the part that shows when finished.

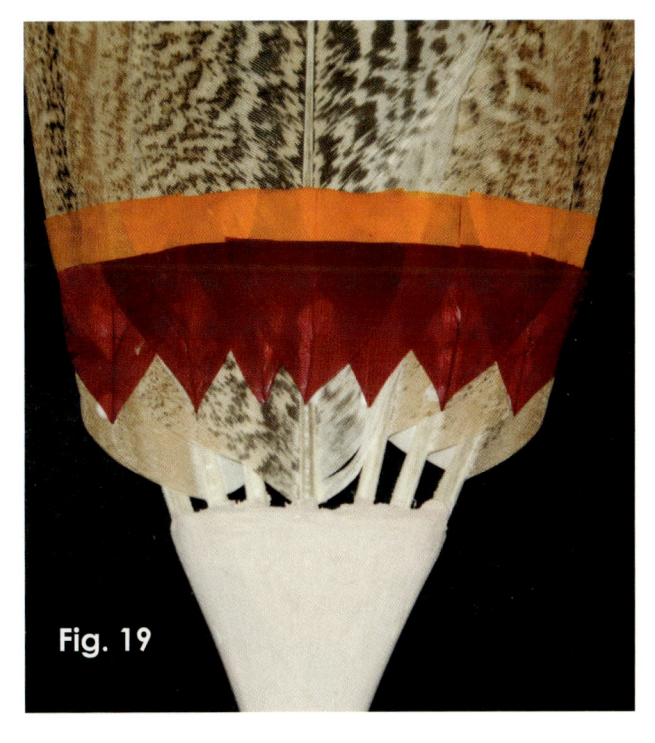

Fig. 19

65

Craftwork Techniques

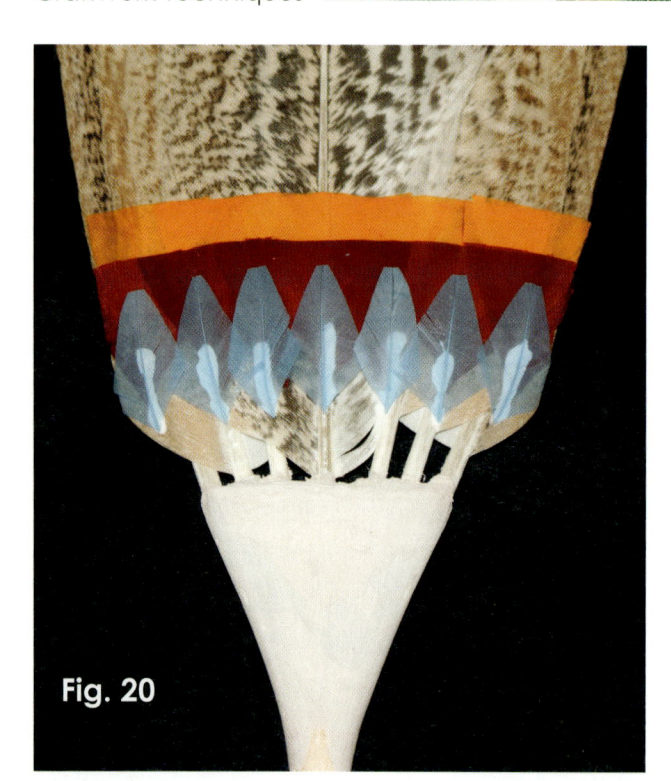

Fig. 20

The third row is made up of 7 goose feathers that have been dyed light blue and then trimmed so that they are shaped like arrowheads. Start by cutting the feather straight across the top, then cut the quill at 1½". Next, cut the slope of each feather so that they are all identical in shape. There is no right or wrong amount of taper as long as it is pleasing to the eye.

This row is laid out starting in the center because the points of the light blue goose feathers need to be precisely placed. Start this only 1/4" below the maroon row because more of the maroon will show due to the taper of the light blue feathers.

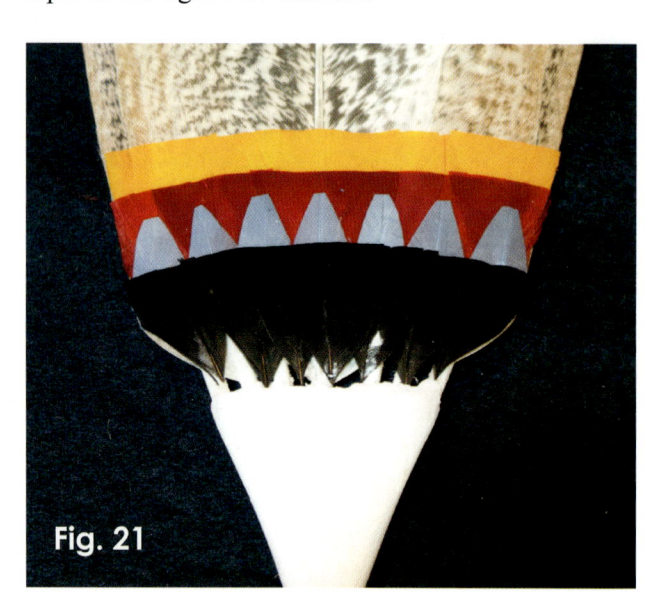

Fig. 21

The fourth row is black and it is cut the same way as rows one and two. On this row, a bit more trimming is required on the two outside feathers as the main feathers taper more abruptly at this point. Glue these in place as before. See **Figure 21**.

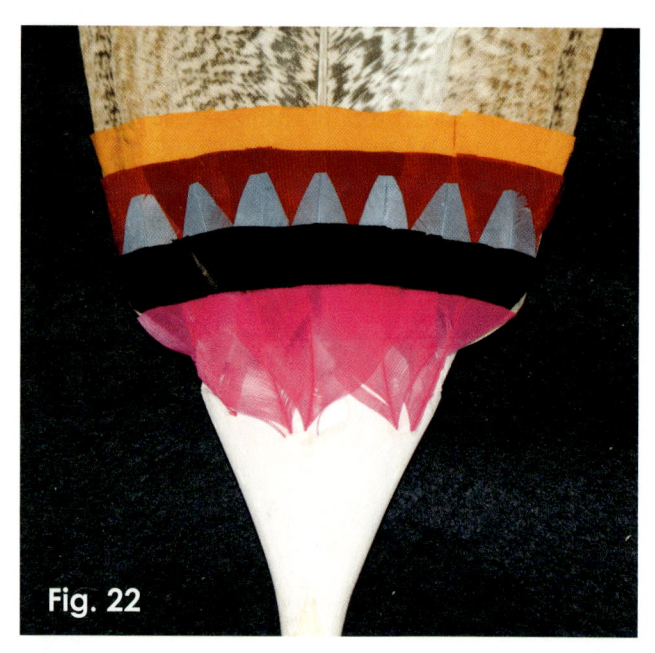

Fig. 22

The fifth and final row is pink, and it is cut a little differently. As with other rows, the outside feathers will need more trimming.

Just as rows one, two and four were cut, trim the tips and base of these in the same way. Each feather will receive two more cuts, straight down about 1/2" from the quill so that they are narrower. They are trimmed in this way because there is less surface area to be covered as the handle tapers in at the bottom.

Attachment of this row is slightly different because the feathers need to be glued to both the other trim feathers and the handle. Their quills will eventually be covered with the leather that covers the handle. See **Figure 22.**

Now the back of the fan should be decorated as well. On older fans, a large plume was often placed in the center of the back, along with decorative feathers placed on either side. I do not recommend cutting the front and back decorative trim feathers at the same time because each row takes some time to glue and dry. Also, pre-cut feathers are easily misplaced, so I make up one row at a time and work on each side independently. I also allow the front side to dry thoroughly overnight before beginning work on the back side.

Flat Fans

Cover the front of the handle only with glue, spreading it evenly. Be sure to use enough glue so that the top edge of the leather is secured to the handle and covers the base of the decorative feathers, but be sure not to let the glue get up into the area of the feathers that will show.

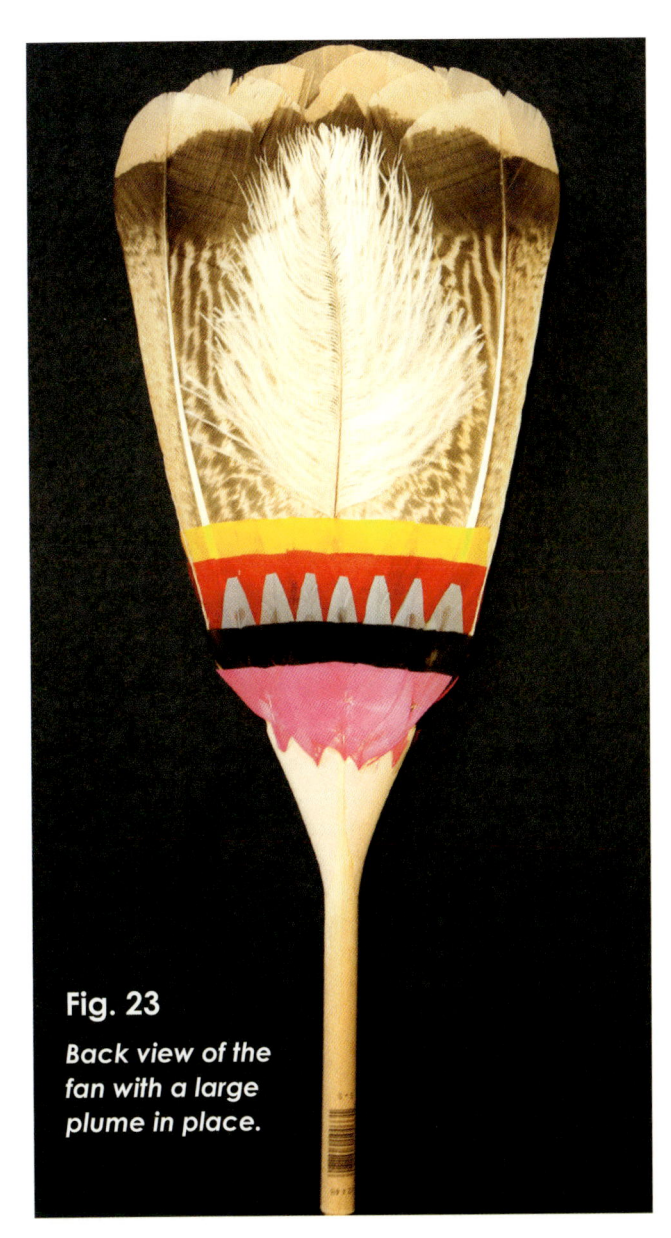

Fig. 23
Back view of the fan with a large plume in place.

Fig. 24

Covering The Handle With Leather

The next step is to cover the fan handle with leather in preparation for beading. Any type of leather can be used, as long as it is fairly thin and can be attached to the handle with the suede, or rough side out. For this fan, I used tanned pig skin, which is not suited for making fringe, but works well for items that will be covered with peyote beadwork. Chamois also works well and can be purchased in the automotive section of large stores. The leather should be stretched, cut and then glued to the handle. Cut a rectangular piece of hide that will more than cover the fan, making sure that the top edge is cut straight across. This process is shown in the next series of photographs, **Figures 24 - 30**.

Craftwork Techniques

Place the glue side of the handle down on the smooth side of the leather and allow it to dry until it is tacky enough that it will not slip. Make sure that the leather is smoothed out, with no wrinkles showing on the front of the fan. Remember, the suede side should be towards the outside!

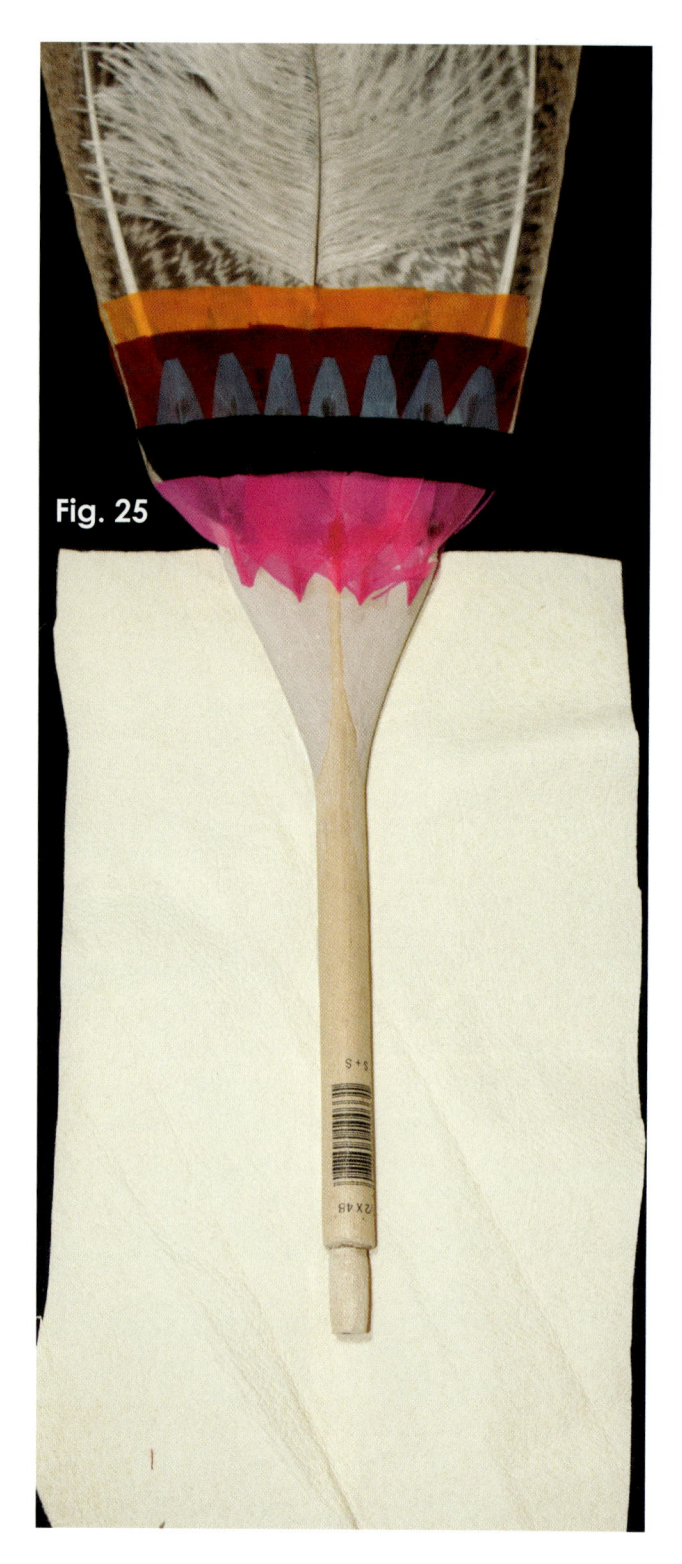

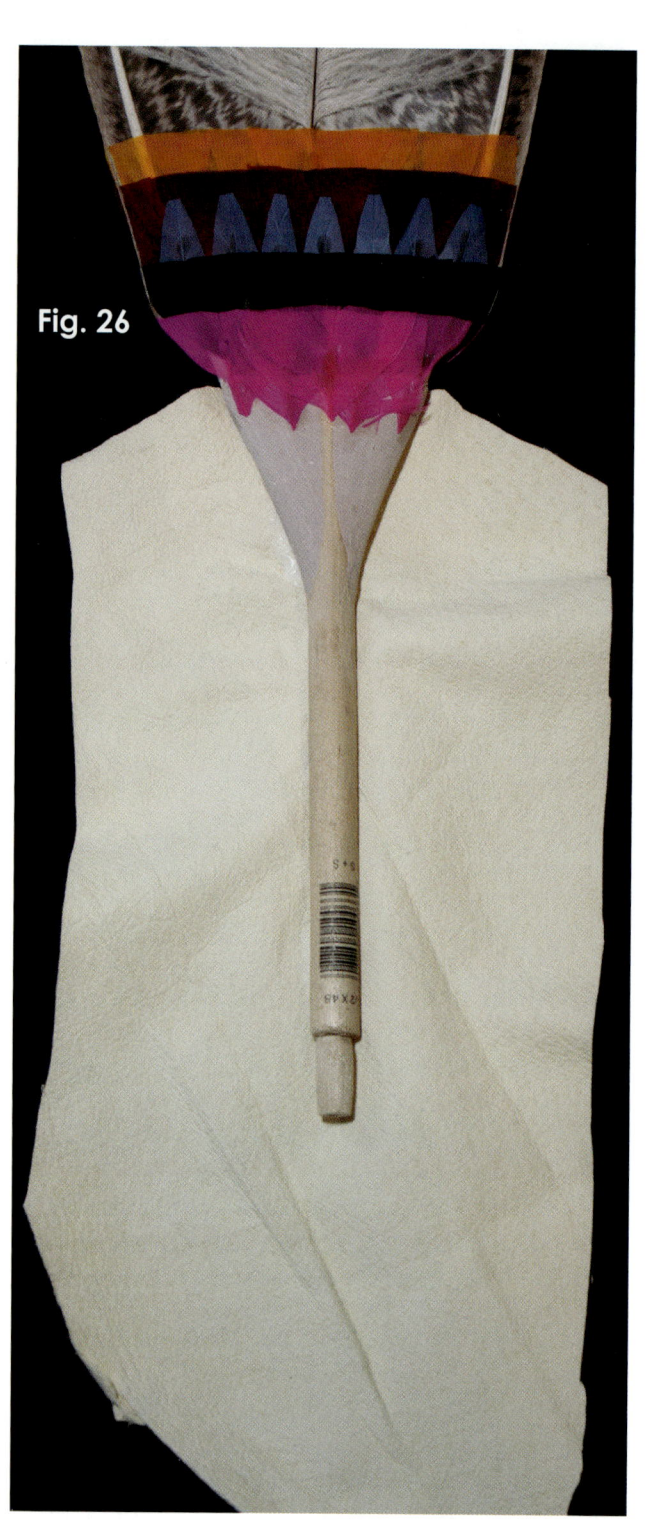

Fig. 25

Fig. 26

Once the glue is fairly dry, the rest of the leather can be attached without disturbing the front side. As the leather is stretched around the fan, you will be able to see the angle along the top where the hide needs to be trimmed. Once this is determined, cut the hide to that angle so that it will be straight across the the back of the fan. See **Figure 26**.

68

Next, cut two slits into the hide at the point where the handle starts to taper into the round section, gently pulling each side of the hide around. Cut just enough to ease some of the stretching, but not all the way to the handle. Also, cut away some of the excess on the sides of the round section of the handle as shown in **Figure 27** below.

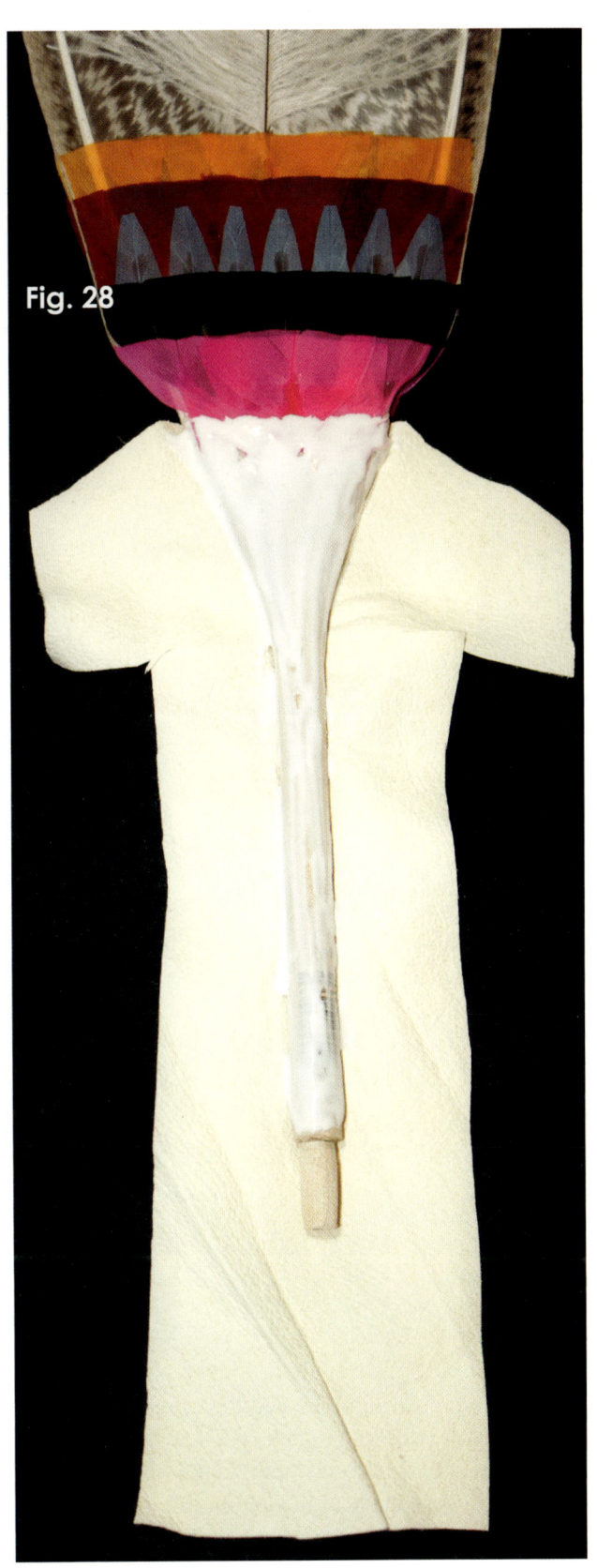

Fig. 27

Fig. 28

Spread a thin layer of glue on the rest of the handle, making sure it is entirely covered except around the peg where the fringe will be attached later.

Craftwork Techniques

Fig. 29

With a pair of sharp scissors, trim off the excess leather, beginning from the point where the fringe will be attached and cutting upward to the top of the handle. The remaining leather will be trimmed off later after the fringe is attached. Once the seam is trimmed, smooth it down so that it lies flat and then let it dry thoroughly.

Another way to attach the leather is to cut 2 pieces of hide in the shape of the handle. Cover the handle with contact cement and allow it to become "shiny", which indicates that it is dry. Cover both pieces of hide with contact cement and allow them to dry as well. Then, place one piece on the front and the other on the back. Pinch the sides with pliers and trim the sides. If the pieces do not quite reach to the bottom of the handle, cut another small piece and using contact cement, wrap it around. This gives the same look as the previous procedure but saves some hide and time.

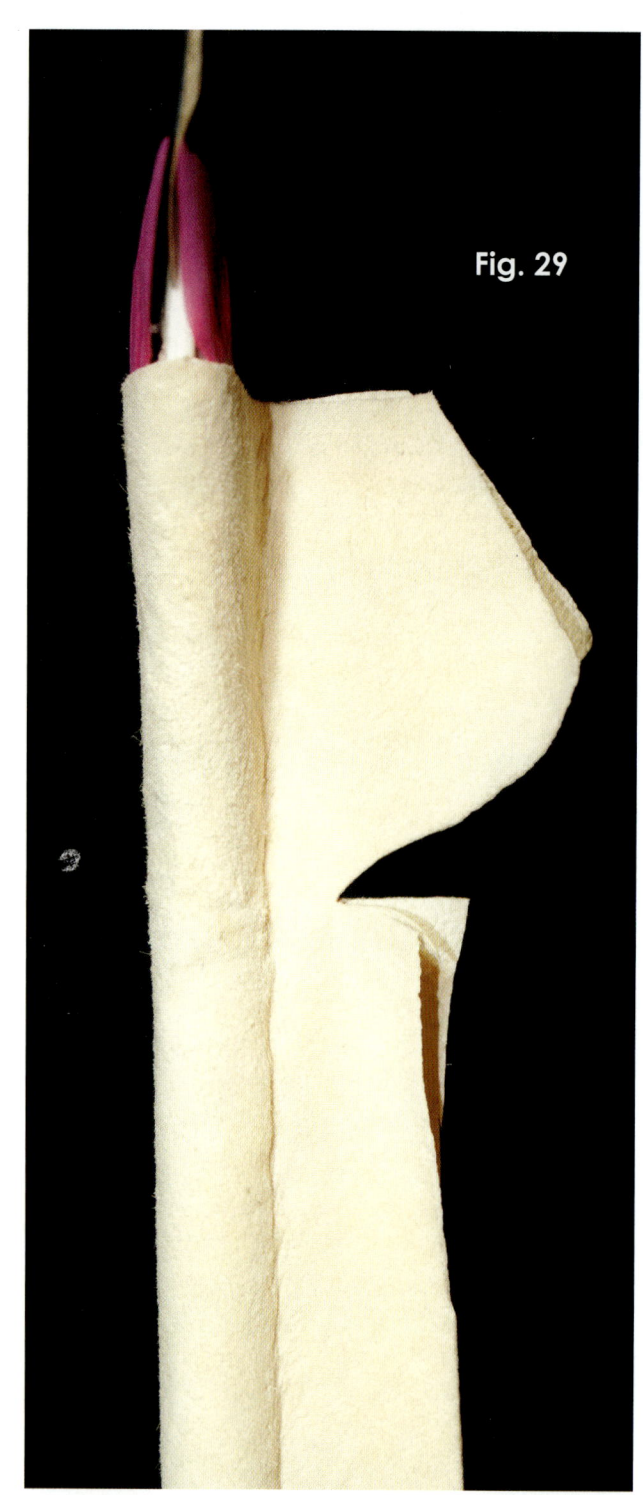

Fig. 30

Stretch the hide around the handle, crimping it together with your fingernails. You can also use a pair of pliers to do this crimping. Note that the area where cuts were made at the beginning of the taper is now separated, which is due to the hide stretching upward. You will also see that the angled cuts at the top of the leather are now straight across the handle. See **Figure 29**. Keep crimping the hide until the glue becomes tacky enough so that it will not slip.

Beading The Fan

This is perhaps the most time consuming part of constructing a fan. Fans can be carried unbeaded after the fringe is attached, but when carrying it this way, the handle is usually covered with a scarf or white handkerchief. However, most dancers prefer to use fans that have beaded handles.

The technique of gourd stitch, or peyote beading as it is sometimes called, has been discussed in a number of books and articles, but we have included some of the "tricks of the trade" here.

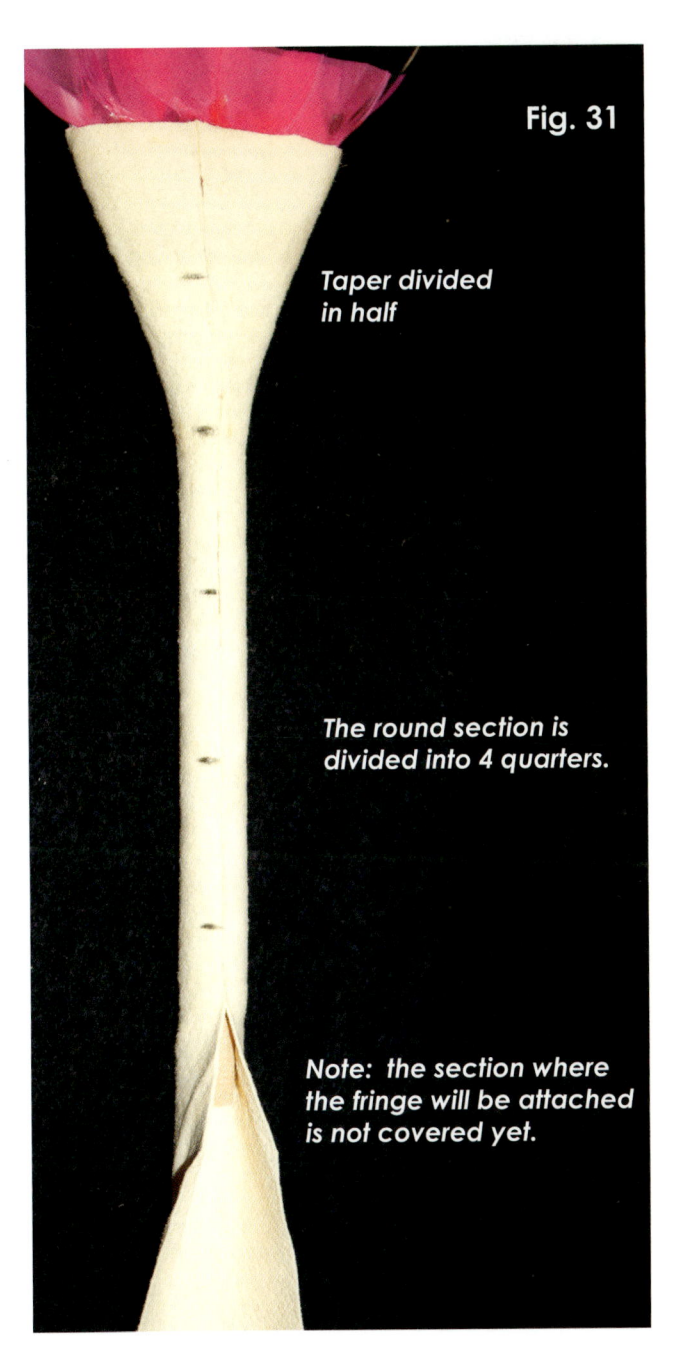

Before the work is started, I prefer to divide the handle into two sections: the upper part, which is tapered, and the bottom part, which is round. Next, divide the top (tapered) section in half and the bottom (round) section into 4 equal parts.

I normally begin the beadwork in the third section of the round part and bead toward the bottom end first. This means I am beading the center section first and working my way toward the fringe. Once the point is reached where the fringe is to be attached, I stop. Turn the fan around and start beading in the other direction, toward the top of the handle where the taper begins. I like to add beads as I move up the tapered section, unlike some craftsmen who like to start at the very top of a fan and bead down toward the fringe. In doing this, beads are dropped instead of being added, but I feel this is a more difficult method.

In order to make the patterns work out properly, the number of beads that encircle the round section of the fan should be a multiple of 3 or 6. A multiple of 6 is better as it allows more design choices; however, a multiple of 3 will still allow you to use many different designs. String enough beads on a thread to go completely around the round section of the handle, count them, and then divide by 3 or 6. If, for example, the number is 31, you should round up to 33. If it is 35, round up to 36. On this fan, the number was 36, which is perfect!

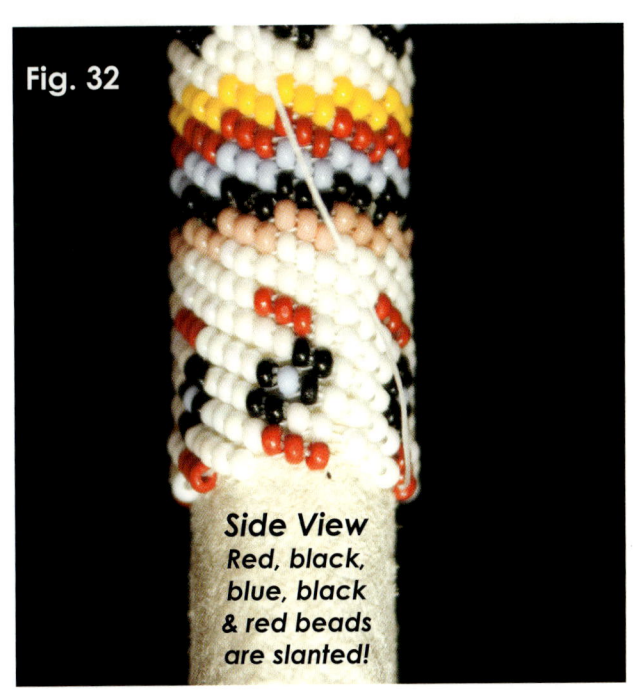

Fig. 31

Taper divided in half

The round section is divided into 4 quarters.

Note: the section where the fringe will be attached is not covered yet.

Fig. 32

Side View
Red, black, blue, black & red beads are slanted!

Craftwork Techniques

The basic gourd stitch beadwork technique is explained more fully with step-by-step instructions and detailed illustrations in *Beadwork Techniques of the Native Americans*, as well as in several other books on beadwork.

The advanced technique discussed here is the addition of the beads as the fan handle tapers outward. As your beadwork progresses up the taper, the beads will begin to spread further and further apart. Note the designs on the front and the side of the handle. The ones on the side are not quite as straight up and down as they are on the front, so extra beads must be added to fill in this space. See **Figures 32 - 34**.

Extra beads are normally added on the sides of the handle or in between 2 designs, as shown here, but always in the area of the background color if possible!

Fig. 34

Fig. 33

Front of Fan Handle color Red, black, blue, black & red beads are running straight up and down the handle!

These extra beads are actually added one at a time, by placing 2 beads where one would normally go, and so on, until a complete "unit" of 3 beads is added. This requires three complete passes around the fan handle. Also, if you add one "unit" on each side of the handle, your design will remain balanced.

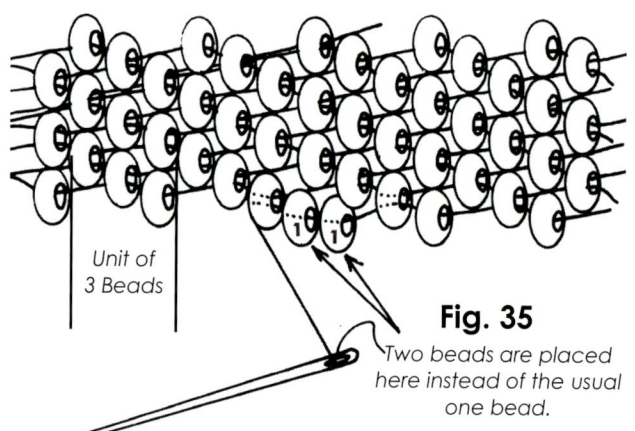

Unit of 3 Beads

Fig. 35
Two beads are placed here instead of the usual one bead.

Adding two beads in the place where one would normally go begins the added unit.

In **Figures 34 and 35**, I have added 2 "units" on each side and between the designs. Note the 2 white beads on the needle, which then goes through the red bead. Then, to add a second "unit" here, 2 more white beads are stitched into the next white bead. **Note:** The thinnest beads available should be selected for adding, as they are easier to fit into the space normally occupied by one bead. Normally, beads like this

72

would not be used, but this is an exception. Likewise, you can select fatter beads to fill wider spaces as the beads first begin to separate on a tapered handle. These would normally be used on the sides of the handle where they would not be as noticeable as they would be on the front.

Fig. 36

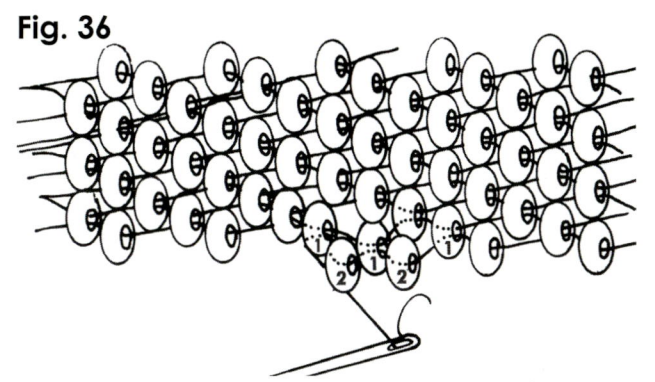

Placing of the second bead of the added unit.

With the second pass around the handle, an extra bead will separate the 2 beads you added on the previous pass. This is the second phase of adding new "units" and is illustrated in **Figure 36**.

Fig. 37

The 2 beads are split in the next step of creating a new "unit" of 3 beads.

Fig. 38

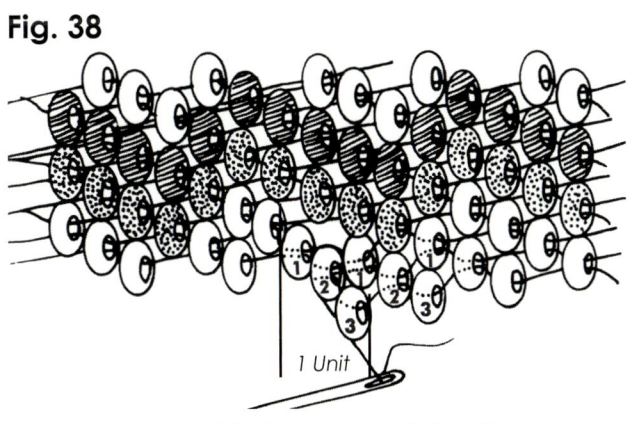

Placement of the third bead, completing the added unit.

The third and final phase, illustrated in **Figure 37**, is the addition of another extra bead, thus completing the full unit of 3 beads. This effectively adds 4 units to the total number of units around the circumference of the fan, giving a total of 48 beads around. You might assume that the rows are now pretty even; however, they actually are not. If you start a new pattern now, you will not make it even part way through before the gaps become too wide on the sides again.

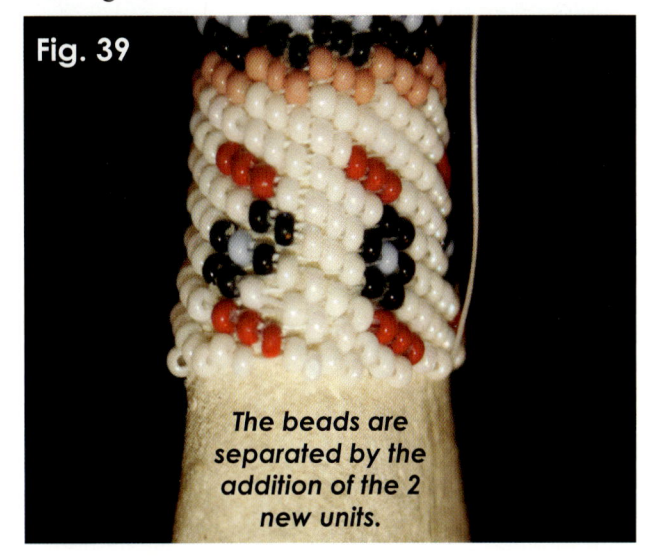

Fig. 39

The beads are separated by the addition of the 2 new units.

For this reason, it is necessary to add 4 more units. This will make the beadwork seem quite crowded but will allow for the next pattern to spread out as you proceed through it. This is done in the same way as the previous units were added, and after the next pattern is completed, units will again have to be added. This process continues as you advance up the tapered part of the handle.

Fig. 40

The second addition of 2 more units on each side of the handle.

Flat Fans

73

Craftwork Techniques

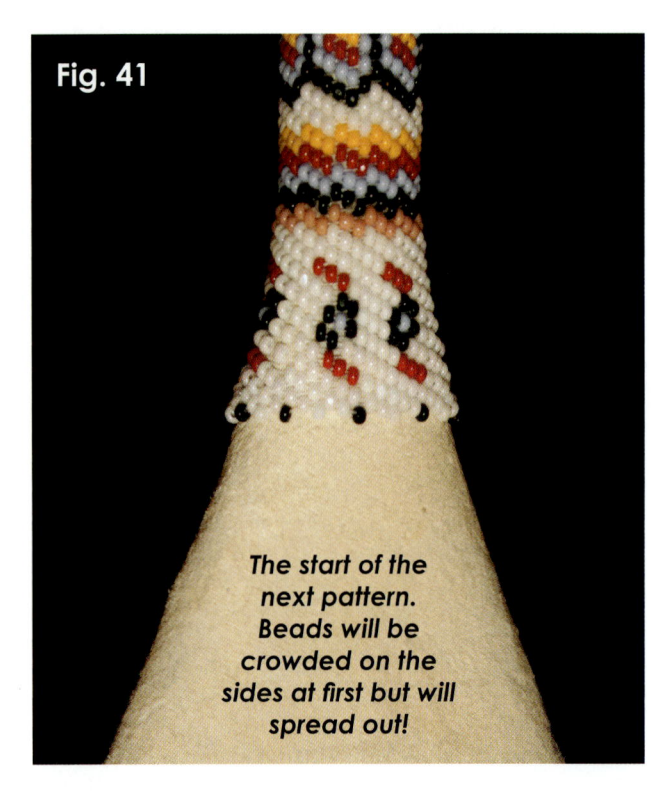

Fig. 41

The start of the next pattern. Beads will be crowded on the sides at first but will spread out!

Continue beading until the entire tapered section is completed. As you work your way close to the top, you will begin to run out of leather in which to tie off your threads. Make sure your thread is long enough to complete the last 4 to 5 rows, as well as having enough extra to be able to run it through the last row one more time. Then, weave it through several more beads to end it. In every white section, except the very top, beads were added in order to keep the patterns even and uniform while tapering up the handle.

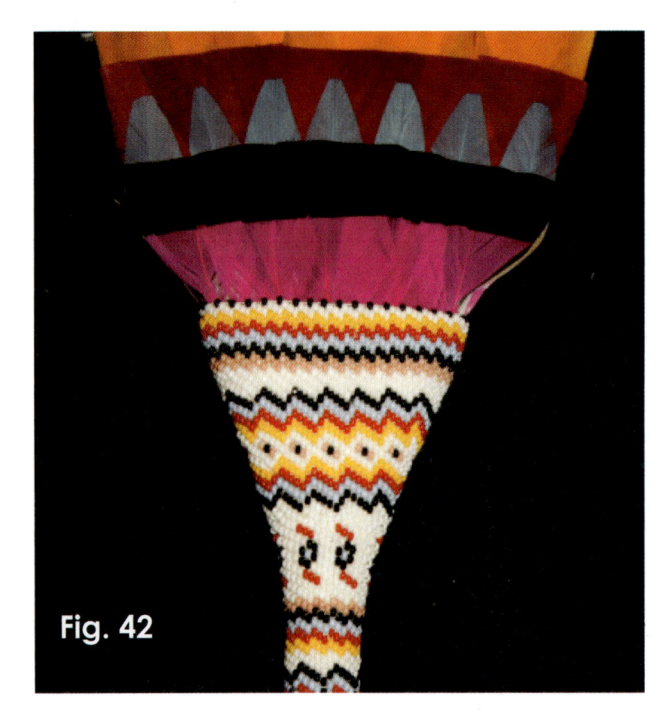

Fig. 42

Fig. 43

74

Some craftworkers like to attach the fringe before they start the beading, and I have done it both ways. However, I have found that it is much easier to bead the handle without the fringe attached, so I add the fringe last and then finish the beading. This keeps the fringe from being handled during the beading process, leaving it nice and white when it is attached. It also keeps it from moving around and getting tangled up with the beading thread.

Note that there is quite a bit of leather at the end of the handle. This provides extra material to work with as we attach the fringe and decide what to do with the excess. You can cut smaller fringes to cover the twisted fringe or cut strips and braid them around the twisted fringe. You could also cut it off and leave a plain edge, or extend it a bit to form a "skirt" which is often edge beaded.

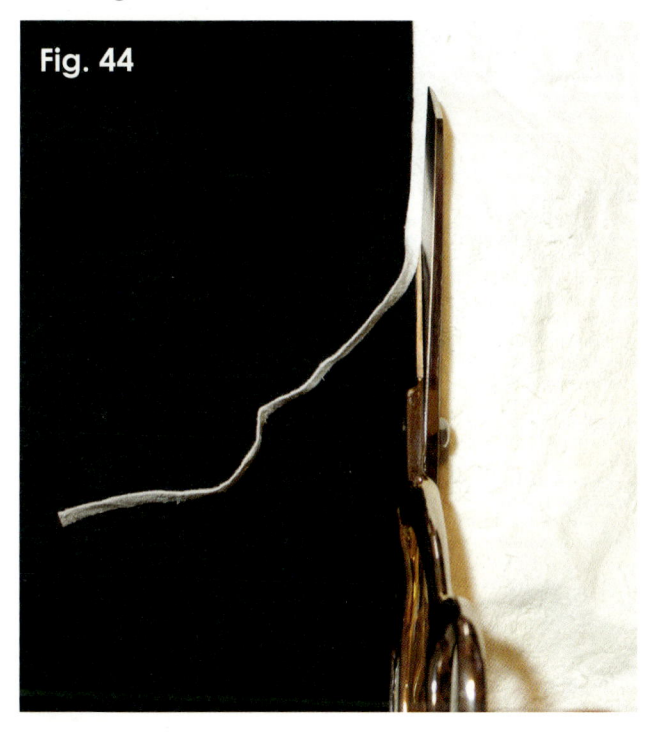

Fig. 44

The "rolled" or "twisted" fringe for the end of the handle is made from narrow strips of leather. Brain tanned deer hide is the best for this as it is thin and very strong. There are a couple of methods that can be used to roll the fringe and the one I like is to hold one end in my teeth and twist the other end with my fingers in the same direction until it is very tight. Don't let it go, either from your teeth or fingers, or you will have to start over. Once it is twisted very tightly, pinch it in the center, bring the ends together, and roll it the opposite direction. Twisting in the opposite direction causes the fringe to twist back upon itself, thus creating the twist, as in a piece of rope.

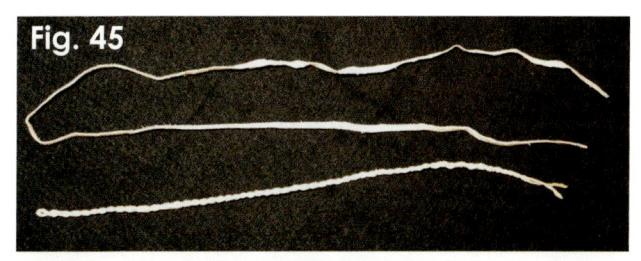

Fig. 45

Continue to roll fringe until you have at least 12 pieces. If the handle is a larger diameter, you may need more than 12 strands. Once all the fringes have been rolled, cut them so that they are all the same length. Finally, put a small amount of glue on the end that has the two tails, smoothing it around to keep the fringe from unraveling. Contact cement also works very well for this step and is not quite as messy.

Fig. 46

To attach the fringes to the handle, pull the leather on the bottom of the fan up and back over the beadwork, exposing the whittled down peg. Cover the peg with glue and begin to lay the fringes around it. Put on the first 5 or 6 strands and let them dry for a few minutes so that when turned over they will not fall off. If needed, add more glue and then attach the remaining fringes. Once they are all attached, wrap this area with Nymo thread. See **Figures 47 - 51**. Cover the thread-wrapped area with a thin layer of glue, securing the fringes tightly to the handle. The leather can now be pulled back down and worked around to cover the fringes, creating a smooth seam. Leave any extra leather as is until the beadwork is completed.

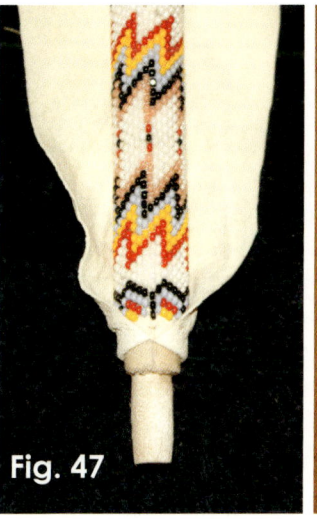

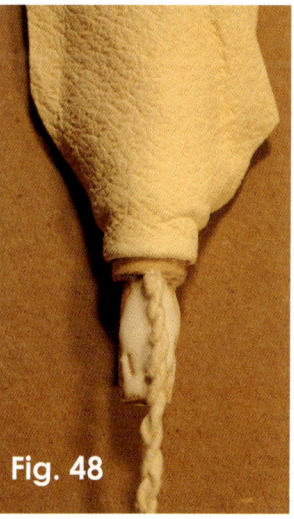

Fig. 47   **Fig. 48**

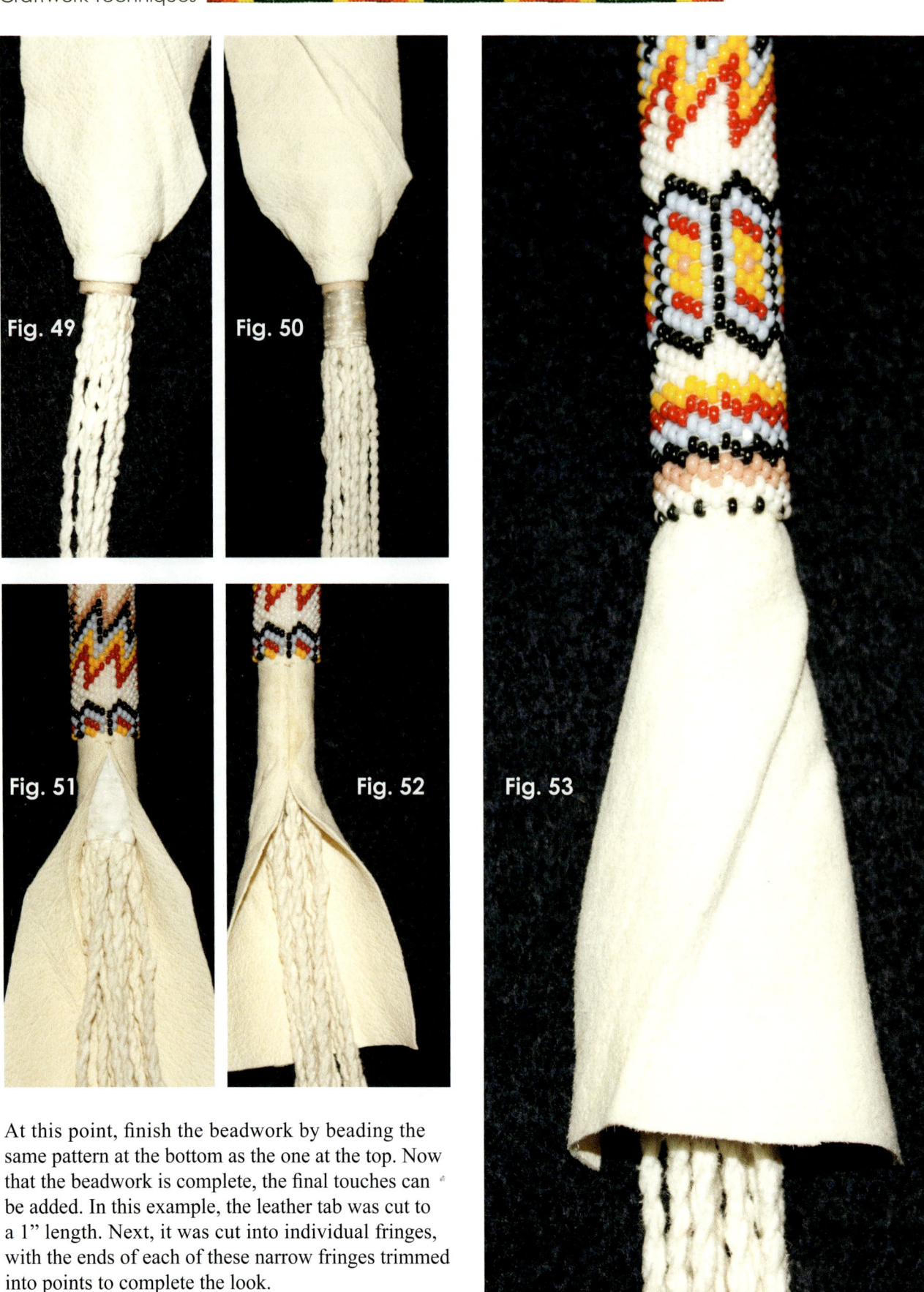

Craftwork Techniques

Fig. 49

Fig. 50

Fig. 51

Fig. 52

Fig. 53

At this point, finish the beadwork by beading the same pattern at the bottom as the one at the top. Now that the beadwork is complete, the final touches can be added. In this example, the leather tab was cut to a 1" length. Next, it was cut into individual fringes, with the ends of each of these narrow fringes trimmed into points to complete the look.

76

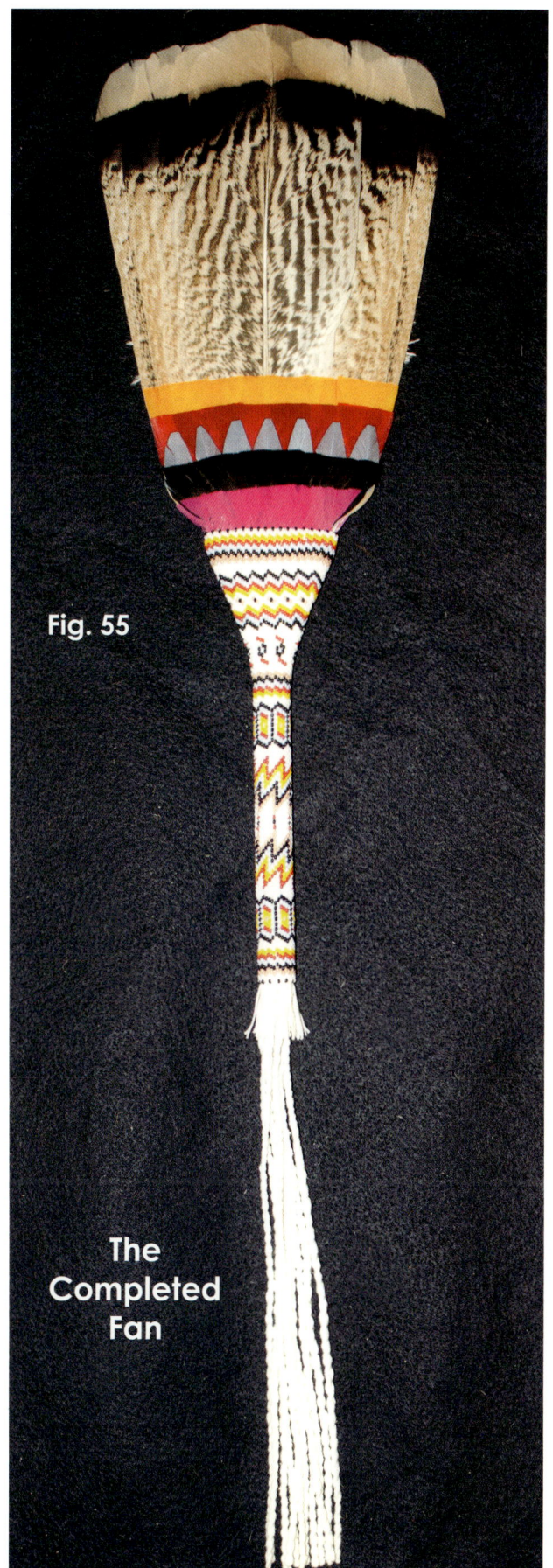

Flat Fans

Fig. 54

Fig. 55

The
Completed
Fan

77

Craftwork Techniques

Feather Extensions & Using Florettes

There are a couple of methods that can be employed in order to extend feathers, of which both techniques are described here. This is not to say that there are not others out there, but these are the two that I use. The one I choose depends on what type of quills the feathers have. Some feathers that have been altered may have little to no actual hollow quills remaining, while others may have nice hollow quills that will allow a different technique to be used.

The first method deals with feathers with little or no quill left. The feathers illustrated here are dyed to replicate the Australian male black cockatoo. As you can see in the photo, the remaining portions of the quills are very short and are not hollow. Therefore, I use "thinwall plastic tubing", which is sem-rigid and can be purchased in different diameters. This is available in 3 foot lengths from Lee's Aquarium & Pet Products (*www.leesaqpet.com*), and I usually keep three sizes on hand. **Do not use the soft plastic tubing** sold in rolls in the plumbing department of home improvement stores as it will not stay straight.

These feathers are too short and have solid quills, so they must be extended using tubing.

Semi-rigid plastic tubing

I like to use Gorilla Glue® for the purpose of attaching the plastic tubing to the feathers. It is a very strong adhesive and makes for a permanent bond, although other glues can be used if you prefer. Gorilla Glue® is activated by water, so placing the glue in the plastic tubing will not begin the drying process. Place a small drop of glue in the tube, then dampen the quill in water and insert it into the plastic tubing up to the bottom of the feather. The moisture from the water on the quill will activate the glue. Let it dry for 2 hours and you will have a permanent bond.

Place some Gorilla Glue® into the tubing, dampen the quill to activate the glue, and insert it into the tube. Then set it aside for the glue to dry. Gorilla Glue® provides a permanent bond.

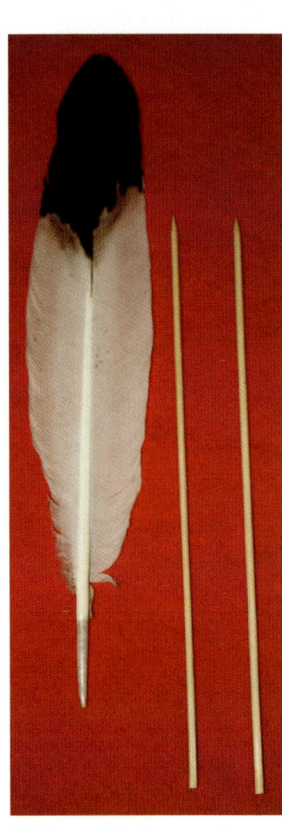

If the quill is in good shape, bamboo skewers can be used to extend the feather.

The second method I like is to use bamboo skewers for the extensions. I use these if I have a nice section of hollow quill. These skewers are used for cooking and are available in two sizes in most grocery stores. Bamboo is strong and flexible, so it is my preferred method for extending this type of quill. The feather shown here is a turkey feather dyed to represent an immature Golden Eagle feather with a full quill.

Flat Fans

The first step is to clip off the tip of the quill. If you can pull out the fibers inside the quill, do so as well, but if you cannot, it is okay to proceed. Again, using clear Gorilla Glue®, put some glue inside the shaft of the feather. Dampen the bamboo skewer and shove it up into the quill as far as it will go. Let it dry for at least 2 hours, and the bond will be permanent. Aleene's Tacky Glue®, wood glue, or carpenter's glue may also be used for this process.

Clip off the tip of the quill and put some Gorilla Glue® inside. Dampen the skewer, insert it into the quill as far as it will go, and let it dry.

Set of Macaw feathers extended with semi-rigid plastic tubing.

Fan set of 10 feathers with extensions completed.

Shown above is the fan set of 10 dyed cockatoo feathers that are ready to have their decorative featherwork added. The ends of the extensions have been trimmed so that all the feathers are the same length.

Shown above is a set of macaw feathers that has been extended using plastic tubing, as the quills had been cut off. Note that these tubes are thinner than the ones used on the cockatoo feathers. These feathers will be used for the purpose of demonstrating more intricate featherwork.

Decorating Techniques

There are many techniques that can be used to add decorative feathers to fans, and these are some of the techniques that I have used. There are many other techniques in use; however, most of these have not been documented and are passed on only by word of mouth. By observing various examples, I have developed techniques that work well for me.

79

Craftwork Techniques

Before you begin, you will need to have a good assortment of different types of small feathers for decorating. These can include pheasant in different varieties, grouse, chicken and rooster hackles, parrot, and, of course, goose florets. Goose florets can be purchased from a number of traders, and you will need a variety of colors, depending on the number of rows of featherwork you want to add.

Some additional supplies you will need are freezer paper, tweezers, Aleene's Tacky Glue®, painter's blue masking tape (not regular masking tape as it is too sticky), ruler, spray sealant in clear matte finish, and very sharp scissors used **only** for cutting feathers.

Steps in preparing small pheasant body feathers for use in decorating the fan. Feathers have been stripped of excess webbing and are ready for sealing.

If using pheasant feathers from a skin, the first step is to pick some feathers from the hide. The photo shows 4 feathers I have pulled, with the first one showing the feather as it comes off the hide. The remaining 3 show the feather after stripping off the excess vane. Leave the long quill on for now as it will be used in the next step.

This step involves sealing the feathers with the clear matte spray. Place a piece of freezer paper on your work surface with the waxy side up. Then place your feathers on the paper, and with a gentle sweeping motion, spray the feathers while either holding the bottoms of the quills or by taping them in place. This should be a light coat of sealant so that the feathers are not sitting in a pool of liquid. The object is to keep the veins of the feather together. Let the feathers dry completely before handling them. It is important to always have good ventilation when doing this as this spray is potent.

After the spray has dried, clip off the quills, and these feathers will be ready for use. They will be used to decorate the center feather which will have several layers of feathers so as to create a special feather that is different from the others in the fan.

Tape the quills down on some wax paper or freezer paper using painters tape. With a sweeping motion, spray the feathers with clear matte sealant and let them dry.

After sealant has dried, clip off bottom of the quill.

Put a spot of Aleene's Tacky Glue® on the back of the feather as shown in the photo. Do not get any glue on the part of the feather that will show. Carefully spread the glue downwards toward the bottom of the feather. A cheap artist's stiff bristle paint brush can be used to spread the glue. You do not want to split the veins of the feather apart at this point.

Spread a small amount of Aleene's Tacky Glue® on the back of the feather, preparing it for application.

80

Stack these 3 feathers on top of one another so that the black tip is touching the previous feather at the black bar. Let these dry while preparing the next layer of feathers you wish to use. In this fan, 3 green dyed Japanese chicken hackles are followed by a white pheasant feather and 3 different red pheasant feathers.

3 yellow pheasant feathers are applied to the center macaw tail feather.

3 chicken hackles are glued on top of the 3 pheasant feathers.

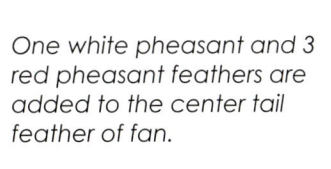

One white pheasant and 3 red pheasant feathers are added to the center tail feather of fan.

The next decorative feathers used on the center feather are goose florets. These are prepped in the same way as the other feathers. A black feather and a yellow one are used for this. Once dry, use sharp scissors to trim the feathers into a blocked "teepee" pattern. The yellow teepee must be smaller than the black one so that it will fit just inside the black one. Following these feathers, a pink dyed grouse feather is the last one applied.

This goose floret was sealed and cut with sharp scissors to create this blocked teepee shape.

Addition of the black teepee goose floret, a yellow floret cut in the same way, and a grouse feather completes the decoration of the center feather.

The next step is to prepare all of the feathers needed to complete the decoration on the quills. For this fan, a layer of white florets with wispy tops, followed by red, orange and yellow feathers are all cut in a zigzag that will give the effect of a diamond pattern. Finally, a long purple feather is used to cover the lower portion of the quill. The following set of photos shows this process of prepping and wrapping the goose florets around the quill. You must prepare enough feathers of each color, and it is always a good idea to have a few extra just in case.

In prepping the florets, if you want a wispy top, use some blue masking tape to cover the top of the floret to protect that part of the feather from the sealant.

Craftwork Techniques

It takes 2 florets to make a nice covering around the feather. So in this case, using 9 feathers, 20 white florets were prepped. Once dry, apply Tacky glue to the back of the floret and lay it on the feather with the center of the floret quill on the **center back** of the macaw feather. Wrap the floret around the feather to the front. Put Tacky glue on the other white floret and place the floret center on the **center front** of the macaw feather. Wrap it around the feather towards the back. One side will overlap the other side. Note that the wisps of the floret are slightly above the base of the feather. It is extremely important that all feathers are treated exactly the same; otherwise, you will not have a clean, even look in the finished product.

All 9 feathers are now wrapped with the first layer of goose florets.

If you want the feather to be fluffy at the top, cover the tip with painters tape as shown, then spray it with the sealant.

The next 3 rows of florets form a diamond pattern using red, orange and yellow. Because these feathers have scalloped edges, there is no overlapping. So you only need 1 nice floret for each layer. These are cut using pinking shears which, again, are only used for feathers. They are cut so that they just barely overlap in the back. For these rows, you do not need long florets, just ones that have a nice center section.

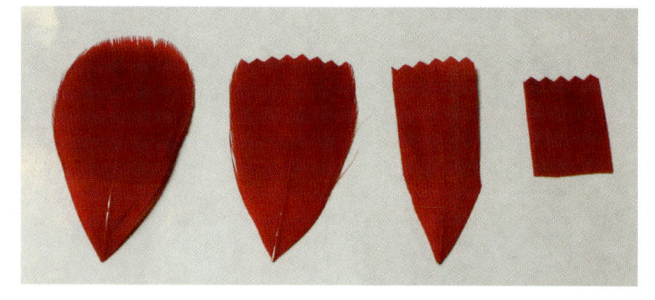

Progression of the preparations for the second row of florets. Sealed, top cut, sides cut, and cut to length.

Spread a small amount Tacky Glue on the back of the floret, keeping it only on the part that has been sealed.

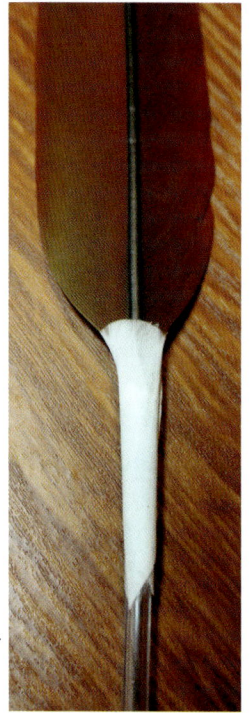

Place the center of the floret on the front of the feather, overlapping the base of the feather by about 1/8". Then, wrap the floret around the quill so that it is nice and smooth, with no wrinkles.

The red florets are cut along the top so that the center point of the zigzag is on the center of the quill. Glue these precisely on the feathers so that they are all in the same position on each feather and on the center front of the quill. The orange florets are cut so that the valley of the zigzag is on the center of the quill. In this way, they can be glued precisely so that a diamond pattern is formed between the red and the orange. See the bottom left photo on the next page. The yellow florets are cut so that the point of the scallop is on the center of the quill, just as the red ones were cut. Glue these on the feather, lining up the point to the valley which will form another diamond between the orange and the yellow. It is okay if the bottom is a bit uneven, as it will be

82

covered later. I used to try to get those perfect as well, which caused me a great deal of grief. Later, when I saw a photo from a great fan maker, I noted that the bottoms were uneven, and realized that at this point is doesn't matter.

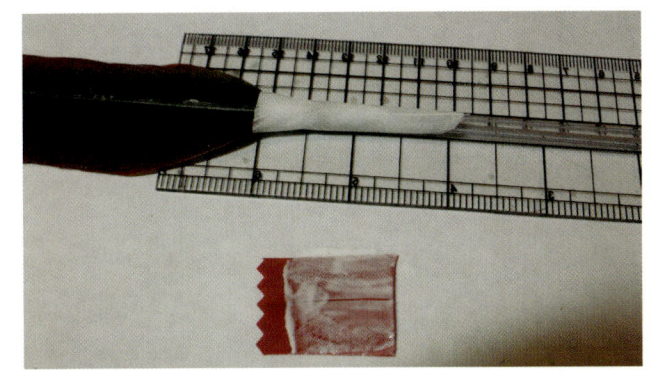

Glue is spread evenly on back of the prepared floret.

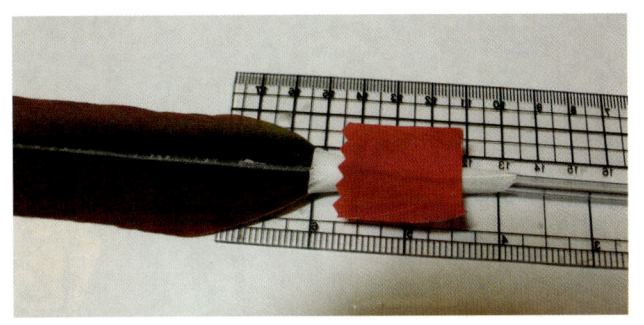

Place the floret on front of the feather at your preferred distance below the white floret. Then, wrap it around to the back of the quill.

Several feathers with the red florets added.

Third row of orange florets have now been added. Note that the orange tops are placed so that the red and orange form red diamonds.

Fourth row of florets are added. Note that the yellow is also staggered to form a row of orange diamonds.

The next row of florets will be the final one, and again, where this row of purple is placed on the yellow feathers is very important. Since this is the major covering of the quill, make sure they all are perfectly even.

The fifth row of florets are added in the same way as others. These are longer as they are the last ones.

83

Craftwork Techniques

The final step of decorating these fan feathers is to add a Japanese chicken hackle to each of the feathers except the center feather. I saved these for last as they are more fragile than the other feathers and cannot be sealed with the spray.

Chicken hackles have been added to the macaw fan feathers.

Leather is added to each feather with a seam on back. It is very important that the leather is accurately placed so that all of the top edges line up when the fan is completed.

To complete these feathers in order to be able to set them in the fan handle, leather coverings and thread wrapping needed to be added. A thin white buckskin hide was used for this purpose. These pieces were cut and fringed before putting them on the feathers. Once again, it is very important that these pieces of leather are at the same height on all the feathers so that, when laid out, they are all even. Glue the leather around the quills, trim it on the back, and sew the seam. The thread wrapping also must be at the same level on each of the quills, as well as the same thickness, so that all the feathers match. Finally, seal the thread wrapping with clear nail polish or super glue.

We highly recommend that you study books, magazine articles and museum pieces for ideas on beadwork designs and colors. In addition, there are literally thousands of photographs and other information now available on the internet for research.

Flat Fans

Thread wrapping ensures closure of the leather in back and that the florets are all tacked down. The thread wrapping is then covered with crazy glue to seal it.

Also, there are several articles on fan making that we highly recommend reading:

Fenner, Earl. ***Moccasin Tracks***, December 1984. Volume 10 number 4. "A Note on Flat Fan Construction", pp. 10-13.

Reddick, Rex. "Flat Fans - A Method Of Construction", ***Wispering Wind***, 2003. Volume 33, Number 4, pp, 4-13.

Stewart, Tyrone. "Modern Flat Fans", ***American Indian Crafts and Culture***, November, 1970. pp.2-5 and p.21.

This is the finished fan, with the handle and fringe attached. (Right Photo)

85

Craftwork Techniques

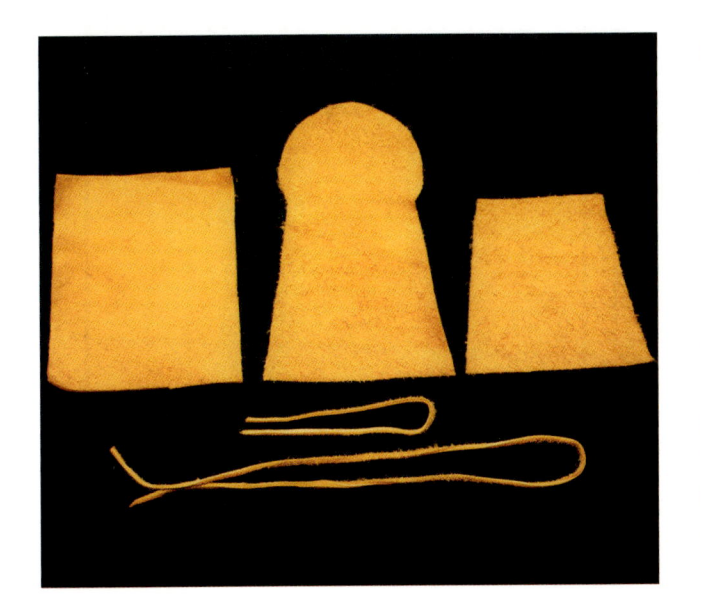

Chapter Eight

Small Dance Bags

When out on the dance floor, it is hard to carry a wallet, so it is nice to have a small dance bag in which to carry your keys and a few bucks. There are many versions of bags that can be made, but for this project, I am making a bag that can be constructed in about 6 hours using simple materials.

Materials

- **Leather:** Commercial or brain tanned buckskin.

- **Needles:** Small Glover's needle in size 9G, and beading needles in size 11 or 12 "Sharps".

- **Beads:** Almost any type of seed bead in size 11/0, 10/0 or 9/0 is a good choice.

- **Spots:** Nickel spots, size 1/8" up to 1/4" work well, and several styles are available.

- **Tools:** Compass for drawing circles & a pen for tracing the pattern on the hide.

Other miscellaneous materials can be utilized as well, but these are optional will be mentioned as they occur in the project.

Cut Out Pattern

First, draw 3 patterns for the bag: a front panel, a back panel and a fringe panel.

If you feel confident in drawing, you can sketch these drawings directly on the hide, but if you are a beginning craftsman, I suggest making paper patterns first.

The bag can vary in size from small to large so it is up to you, but it should be based on the items you plan to carry in it. *Caution:* If you make the bag too small, you won't be able to get your fingers in it.

Fig. 1

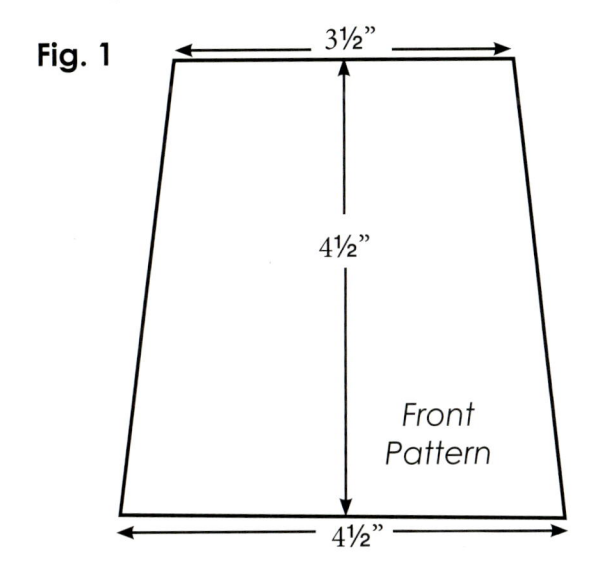

Front Pattern

3½"
4½"
4½"

Craftwork Techniques

The back panel will have the same dimensions as the front panel, with an additional area that will become the flap. **See the drawing below**.

There is a dot placed in the center of the flap, and this is used to construct the circular outline of the flap with a compass. If desired, it can be placed higher on the flap, and the farther up it is placed, the larger the flap will be. Place the point of the compass on the dot and the tip of the pencil on the top corner of the bag panel. Then draw an arc to the other side, which will create the outline of the flap.

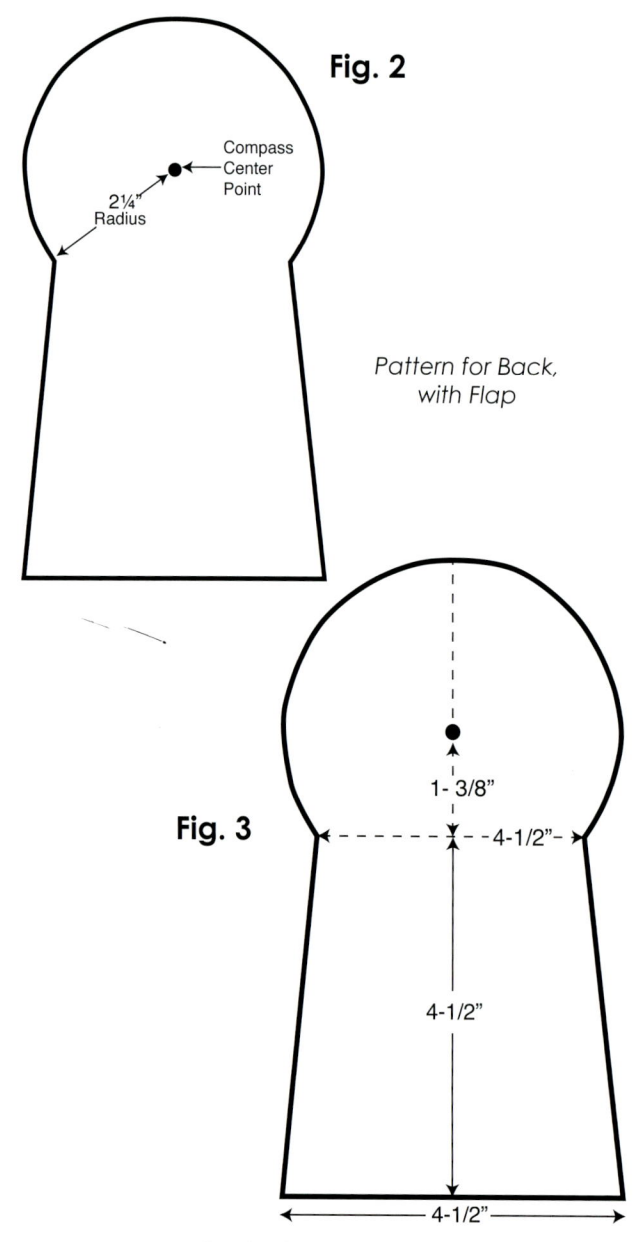

Fig. 2

2¼" Radius
Compass Center Point

Pattern for Back, with Flap

Fig. 3

1-3/8"
4-1/2"
4-1/2"
4-1/2"

Draw a pattern for the fringe that is the same width as the front and back panels, or 4-1/2" in this case. The length can be as long or short as you desire, as this is simply a matter of personal taste.

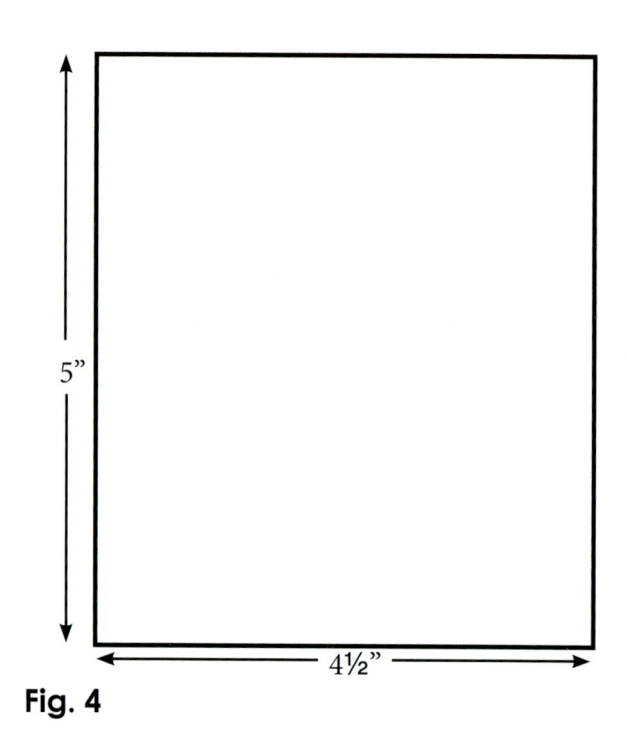

5"
4½"

Fig. 4

Cut Out The Leather

Once the patterns are drawn, trace them onto the hide you are going to use. Make sure your markings are on the inside of each panel! While you are cutting, also cut two laces as shown in **Figure 5**.

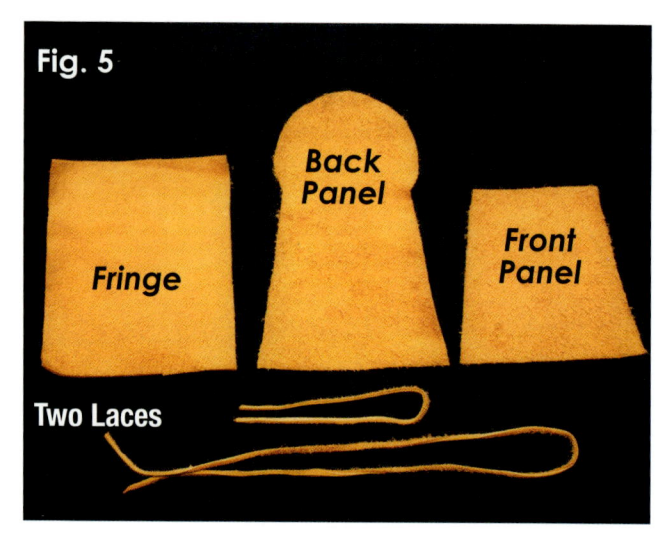

Fig. 5

Fringe
Back Panel
Front Panel
Two Laces

88

Small Dance Bags

Fig. 6

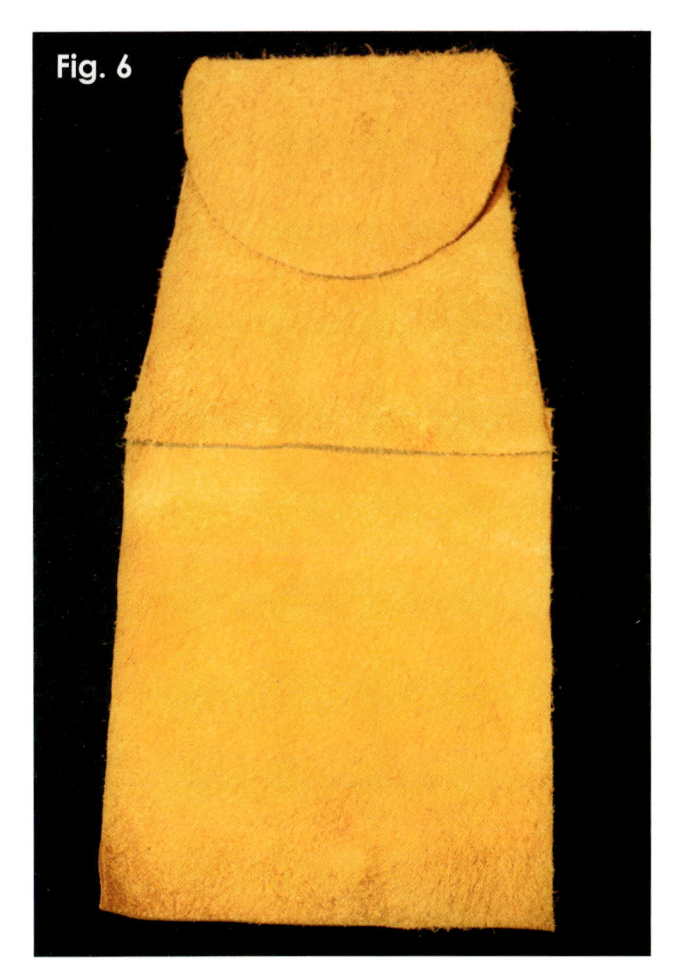

The three pieces as they will look in the finished bag.

For demonstration purposes, all three pieces are laid out in **Figures 5&6** to show how they will be assembled and how the finished product will look.

Sewing The Pieces Together Starting With The Bottom Seam

Split a piece of simulated sinew a couple of times and thread a Glover's needle with one of these strands. Put the three pieces of the bag together so that the insides face each other and the fringe is in between them. The rough sides should be on the outside of the bag. Start stitching the bottom of the bag from the back toward the front about 1/8" from the bottom edge. Using a running stitch (going up and down through the leather) about 1/8 inch apart, sew completely across the bottom. When you reach the other side, sew back in the opposite direction so that the stitches are opposite one another. This will give the appearance as if the stitches were made with a sewing machine. **See Figures 8 & 9**.

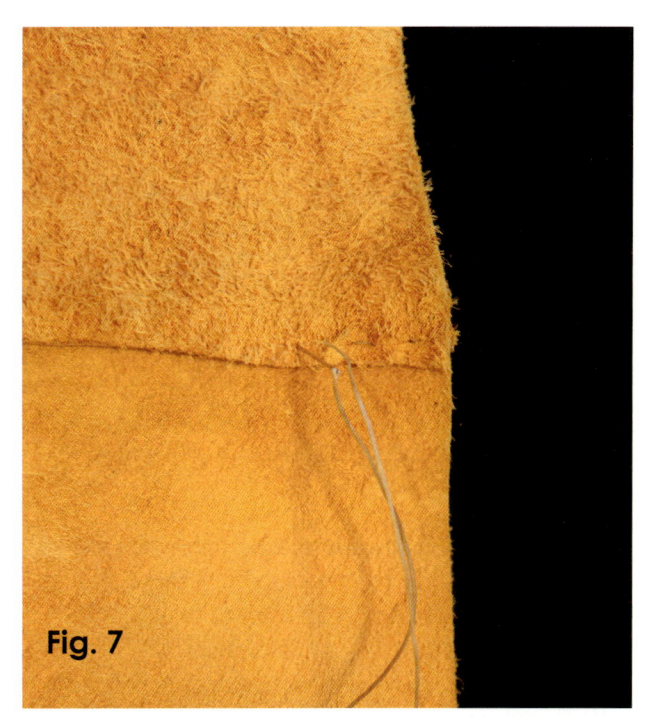

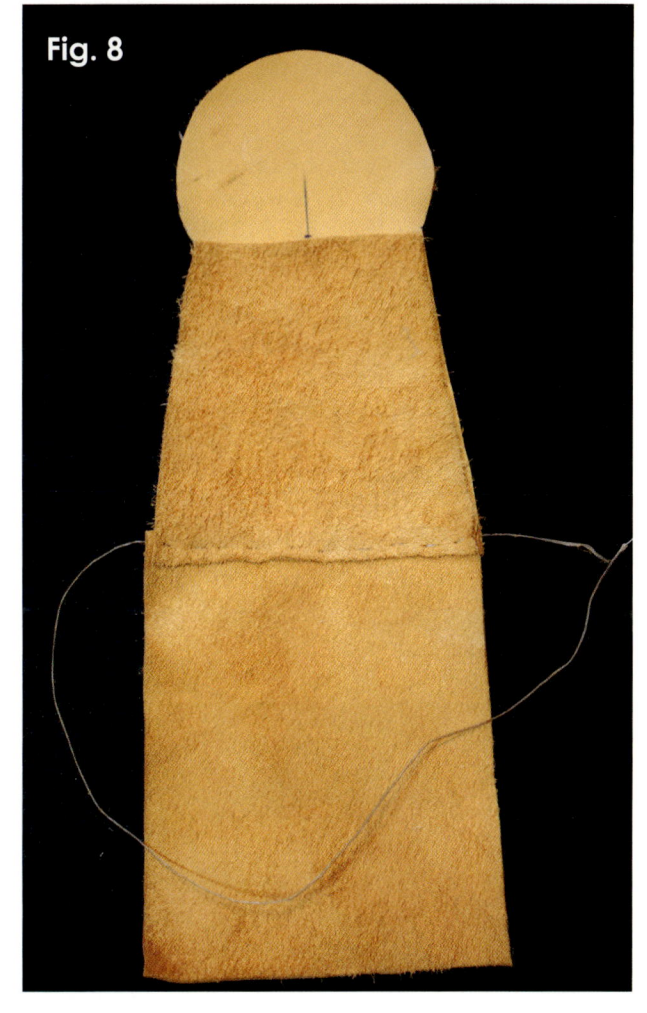

Fig. 7

Fig. 8

The first running stitch is completed across the bottom of the bag, securing the fringe.

Craftwork Techniques

Fig. 9

View of the stitching after returning to the starting point and knotting the end.

Once you have reached the starting point, tie the two ends together. It helps to carefully melt these ends so that they do not come apart. Twist the two ends of the sinew together, and using a lighter, heat the knotted ends of the sinew until they begin to melt. When the melted area gets close to the end, flatten it out with the end of the lighter, thus melting it all together.

Sewing The Side Seams

Using one of the picot edge beading techniques described in **Beadwork Techniques of the Native Americans**, sew the sides of the bag together. Thread a "Sharps" needle with size D Nymo thread, waxing it thoroughly. Begin stitching through the back and front panels at the point where the fringe was sewn to these two pieces. Place 3 beads on the needle and then stitch back through both of the panels, about ½ bead space away from your first stitch. Then go back through the last bead, which will cause that bead to lie on its side, as shown in **Figure 10**. Next, put 2 beads on the needle and make the same stitch again, causing the first bead to stand up between the 2 flat beads. The second bead will become the next flat bead, and so on.

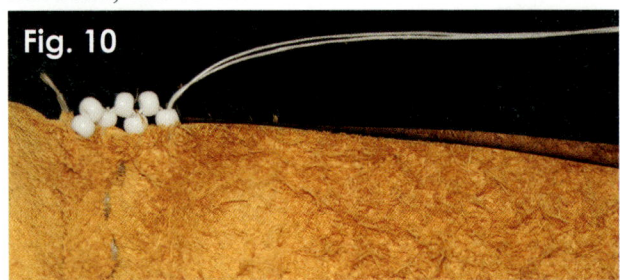

Fig. 10

The sides of the bag are joined using the edge beading technique. This edging will eventually be connected to the edging on the flap.

Fig. 11

The end of the knot is melted to prevent raveling.

Continue in this manner until the entire side seam is completed. When you reach the end of the seam, tie off the end of the thread inside the bag.

Repeat this same process of edge beading for the other side of the bag. This will complete the beading along both sides of the bag, thus joining the sides together. Later, this same type of picot edging will be added around the outside edge of the flap and along the bottom edge of the bag. This will be connected to the picot beading along the edges.

Fig. 12

Both side seams are now sewn together.

Small Dance Bags

Decorating The Bag

The next step is decorating the bag, and there are a number of different methods and materials that can be used to enhance it. Some of these include the use of nickel spots, tin cones and various combinations of beadwork. For this bag, I have chosen to use nickel spots and a beaded panel, although I could just as easily have used tin cones around the flap and a medallion on the front panel or on the flap instead. Another variation would be to use a silver concho or an abalone shell button on the flap. So you can see that there are many different combinations possible, and these choices are based on individual preferences.

I am using 1/4" diameter nickel spots, and to attach these to the flap, I start at the center as shown in **Figure 13**. Working from the inside of the flap, locate the center point, about ½" in from the edge. Then, using a hole punch, place two small holes ¼" apart. From the front side of the leather, insert the two prongs of the spot and fold them over to secure them in place.

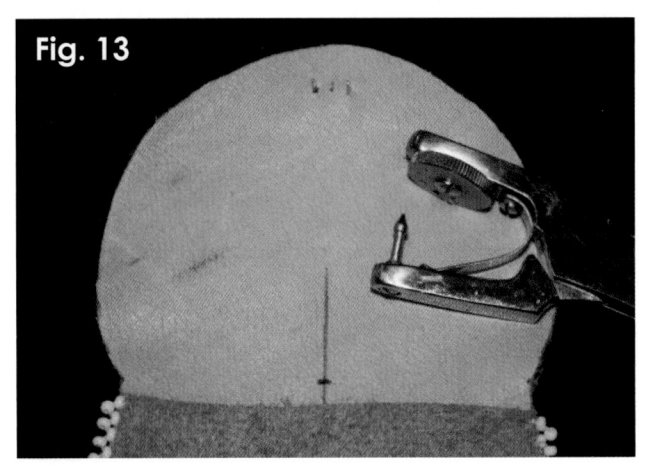

Fig. 13

Two holes are punched in the center of the flap for attaching the nickel spots.

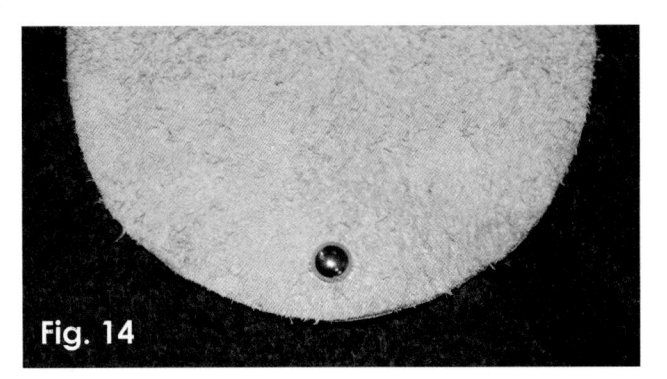

Fig. 14

Front view of the flap showing the first silver spot after it is attached.

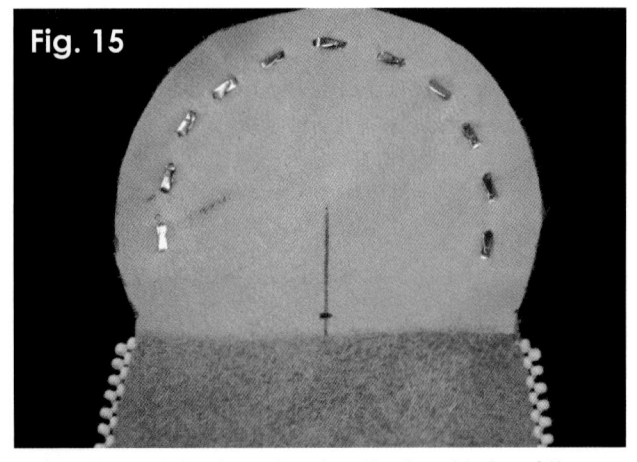

Fig. 15

Inside view of the flap showing the bent tabs of the spots securing them in place.

Continue placing the spots evenly around the flap. I like to make the space between the spots equal to their width, or diameter. Do not put them too close to the point where the flap folds over, as this will not allow the flap to lay flat.

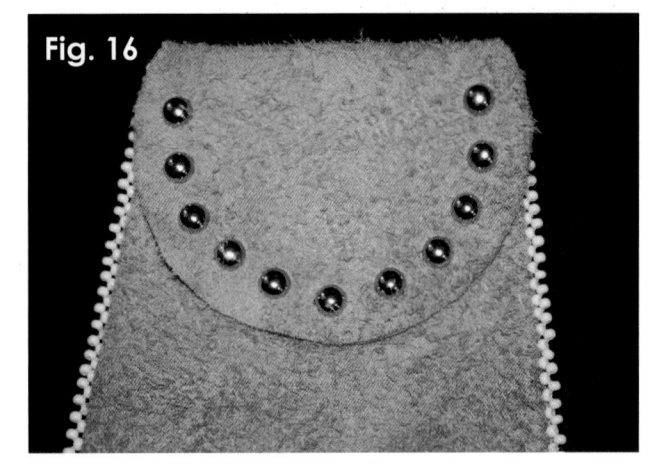

Fig. 16

Front view of the flap showing the spots in place.

Attaching Tin Cones

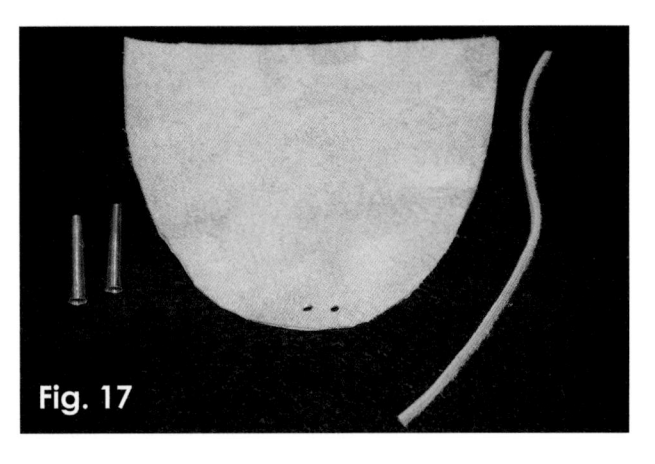

Fig. 17

91

Craftwork Techniques

If you prefer to decorate your bag using tin cones around the flap, **Figures 17-22** show the method I use. These can be used instead of, or along with, the edge beading, but this decoration is entirely up to you. Begin by punching holes close to the edge of the leather, about 1 cone apart from each other so that they will be attached fairly close together.

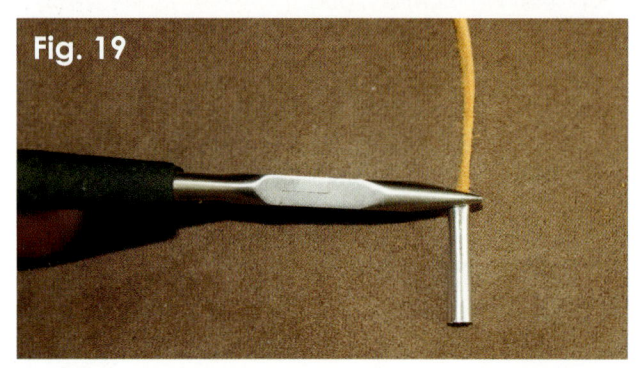

Fig. 18

Fig. 19

Tie a knot in the end of the thong and insert it through the cone. Pull the thong into the cone and crimp it with needle nose pliers as shown in **Figure 19**. Run the thong through the flap and place a second cone on the loose end of the thong. Slide it up and securely crimp it with the pliers, as before. *Note:* Do not pull these too tightly. If you do, they will flare out to the sides instead of hanging down properly. If the cones are not securely crimped, they may fall off.

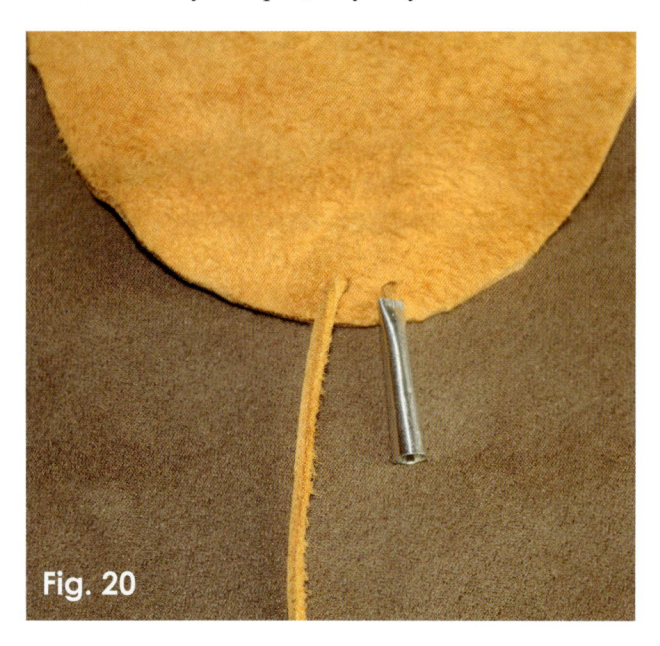

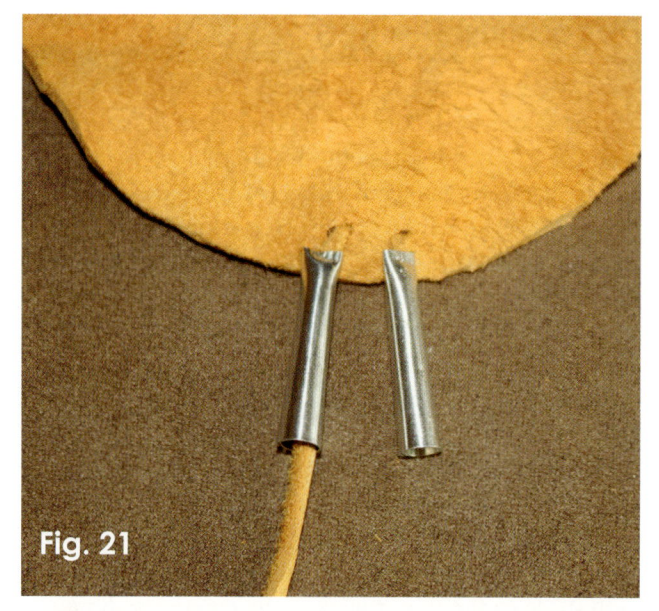

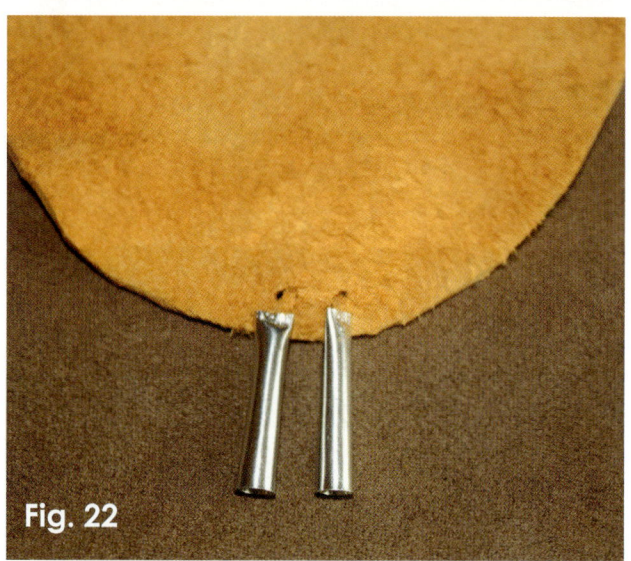

Fig. 20

Fig. 21

Fig. 22

I wanted to provide a nice contrast with the white beads and silver spots, so I used red beads for the edging on the flap. To make a smooth transition from the white edge work to the red, it is quite easy to "connect" these sections. Thread a beading needle, knot it and to hide the knot, stitch through the hide from inside the bag. Bring the needle up through the last white bead from the side seam and then, continue the edge beading around the flap using red beads. When you reach the other side, go down through the top white bead and tie off the thread inside the bag.

Use this same method to complete the bottom row of edge work. This time though, the knot can be on the back side of the bag in order to hide it.

Small Dance Bags

Fig. 23

Flap edge work connected to side edge work.

Side edge work connected to bottom edge work.

The next step is cutting the fringe. This is easily done using a sharp pair of scissors, which I prefer. However, some craftsmen prefer to use an X-Acto® knife and ruler to do this. Regardless of the method you use, do not mark the lines to cut, as you will not be able to hide them. With some practice, the fringe can be cut in a uniform, even width.

Fig. 25

To decorate the front of this bag, I decided to do a beadwork panel in lazy stitch. Start in the center on the bottom and add as much beadwork as you desire. Most of the top area of the bag will be covered by the flap, so only 3 lanes of beadwork were needed. The design is a very simple, reverse tipi pattern.

Fig. 24

A 12" long tie thong is cut from the same buckskin used for the bag, and this is now attached by punching 2 holes along the fold in the flap. These are shown in the photo of the finished bag and can be used to tie it to your belt or dance stick, or to slip around your hand for carrying it that way.

Fig. 26

The Finished Dance Bag.

93

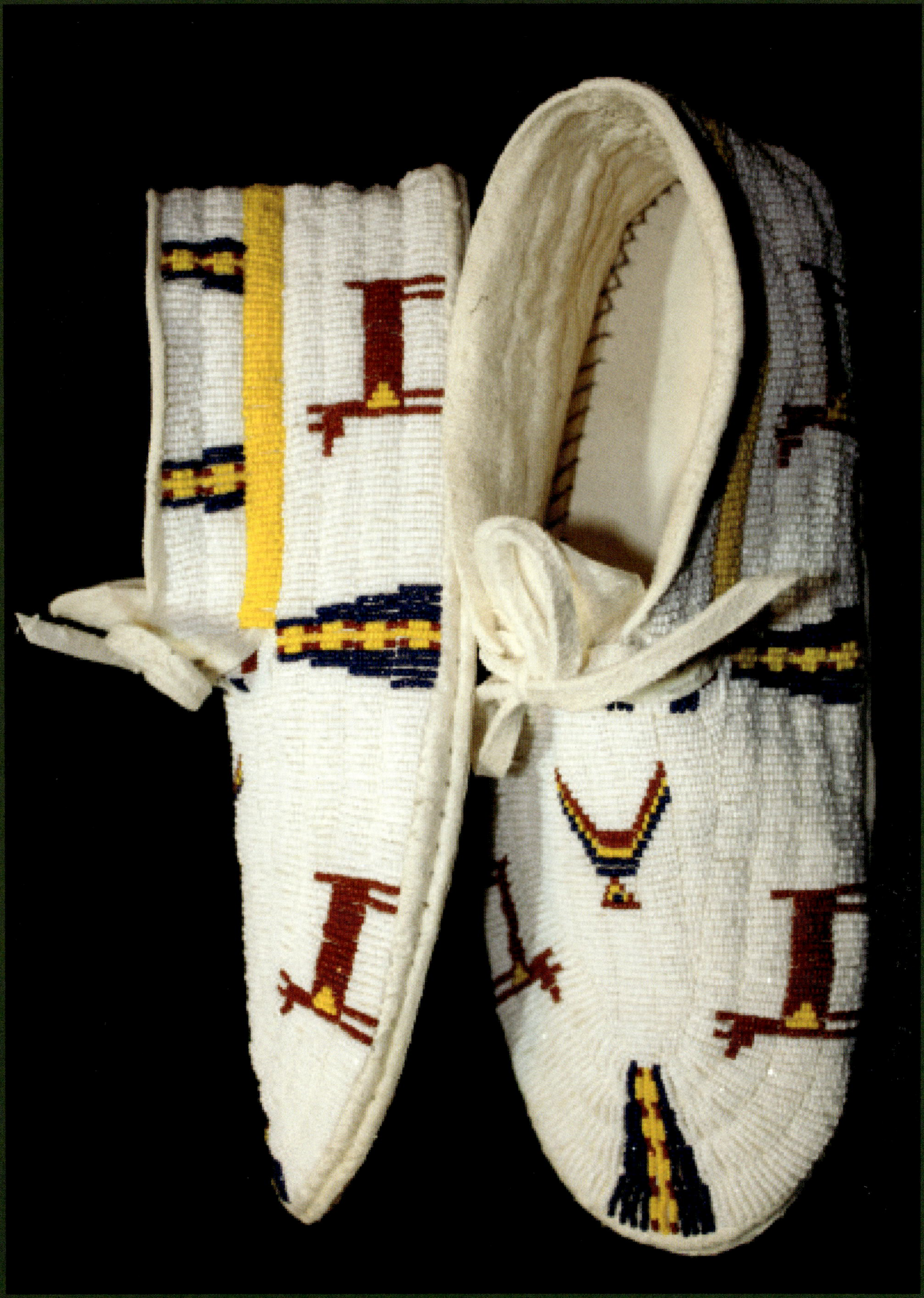

Chapter Nine

Moccasins

There are many types of moccasins and those from different tribes or groups each have their own, unique characteristics. "Plains Hard Sole" is the style of moccasin constructed in this chapter, using Cheyenne design elements in the beadwork. Based on my observations from attending modern powwows in the traditions of both the Southern and Northern Plains, this is the style of moccasin that is most often seen being worn. While moccasins often seem to be one of the last articles of regalia that dancers construct or acquire, they add the final, finishing touches to the overall appearance! Many people are intimidated by moccasin construction. The goal of this chapter is to present instructions that will encourage you to tackle this project and complete a nice pair of Cheyenne style moccasins.

The two most important materials for moccasins are buckskin for the uppers and latigo or rawhide for the soles. Based on years of experience making over 200 pairs of moccasins, I can testify that using poor quality hide makes a poor quality moccasin. Many years ago when I was only 16 years old, I made a pair of moccasins from some hide that was sold as "like brain tan", but it was more like Chamois than buckskin. I was a new craftsman and didn't know any better. At the time, no one told me any differently, but I really wish they had! After spending hours beading these moccasins, I put soles on them and wore them to a powwow. Although they looked beautiful, they tore after only one dance. What a disappointment this was, but it was a lesson learned, and I have never used cheap hide since. Now, I only use brain tanned buckskin as it is the best and easiest to bead on. There are also commercially tanned hides that are good substitutes for brain tanned, and these are carried by a number of traders. One of the best is "German Tanned" buckskin, which works very well. It has much the same qualities as brain tanned because it is prepared using a similar process, and it is sueded on both sides. However, one should avoid split hides such as suede. Although both sides are rough like brain tanned, they are not as strong and will not hold up as well for moccasins.

Materials

- **Buckskin for Moccasin Uppers**
- **Rawhide or Latigo for Soles**
- **Sharp Scissors** - *Gingher* brand, in both large & small sizes.
- **Hole Punch**
- **Sharp Awl**
- **Real Sinew or Imitation Sinew**
- **Beading Thread** - Size D Nymo.
- **Beading Needles** - 11 or 12 Sharps.
- **Glover Needles** "J" curved type in a medium size.
- **Beads** - 11/0, 12/0 & 13/0 are the most popular.
- **Beeswax**
- **Paper, Pencil & Ruler** - Butcher Paper or a Grocery Bag for drawing patterns.

Craftwork Techniques

Moccasin soles should be thick, but not so thick as to be inflexible. I have used two types: hand prepared rawhide and commercially tanned latigo, which I prefer in white. This type of rawhide is not really "raw" like the yellowish kind used for some drums and rattles. It is processed using a brain solution that is rubbed into the flesh side of the hide, with the hair often left on. It is then left to dry into a flexible form versus being worked like buckskin to make it completely soft. In the old days, soles were often made from the smoke flap portions of old buffalo hide teepee covers. The constant smoking made the hide water resistant and thus, well-suited for moccasins. Since most of us don't have access to buffalo hide smoke flaps, we must obtain our rawhide from other sources, and several traders carry rawhide and latigo soles. Regardless of the sole material you choose, it should be about 1/8" thick. If it is much thicker than this, you will not be able to turn the moccasin right side out after the sole is attached.

The first, and most important step, is to make a pattern for the moccasin that will fit your foot. Some students of Indian lore will tell you that certain tribes made moccasins with a sole that was uniquely their own shape. I feel differently about this and suggest that Indians, just as anyone else, have feet which are shaped based on their genetics. Therefore, I believe that Crow moccasins should have a curved sole, not because it is "authentic", but because that was the foot shape of the Crow people! So, I recommend that you make your pattern to fit your foot.

Begin the pattern for the upper by taking the following measurements: the distance from your toe to your heel, the distance from your toe to the center of your arch, and the distance across the top of your instep at the arch. This last measurement is taken from the floor on one side to the floor on the other, as shown in **Figure 1**. With these three measurements, anyone can make an upper that fits!

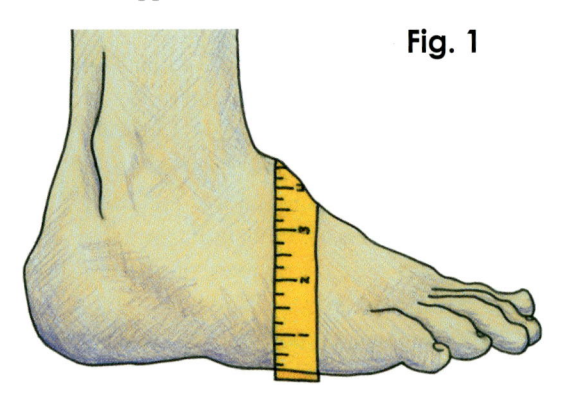

Fig. 1

Add 1" to your first measurement, from the toe to the heel. This will be the length of a box you will draw, as shown in the "Moccasin Pattern" illustration below. This works for both narrow and regular width feet, but if your foot is extra wide, add 1½" to this measurement. The width of the rectangle is 1½" to 2" narrower than the length, depending on whether your foot is normal or wide.

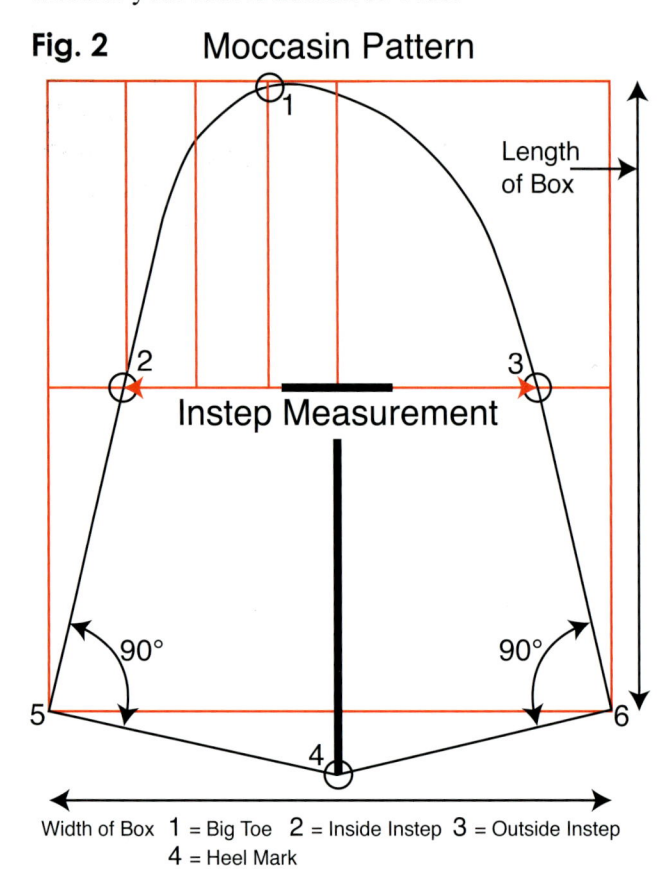

Fig. 2 Moccasin Pattern

Width of Box 1 = Big Toe 2 = Inside Instep 3 = Outside Instep
4 = Heel Mark

Once you have the rectangle drawn, divide it into 4 equal quarters. Now divide the top left quarter of the rectangle lengthwise into 4 equal parts. The top of the first line to the left of center is labeled as Point 1. The third line over is labeled Point 2 where it meets the line that divides the full rectangle in half. Add 1/2" to the measurement from across your instep and use this distance to determine Point 3 on the right side of the center line. For most men's feet in sizes 9-11, this distance is usually about 7" to 7-1/2". The measurement from your toe to the top of your instep is the point at which the "T" starts. These points are all shown in **Figure 2**.

From the bottom left corner of the rectangle (Point 5), draw a straight line intersecting Point 2 and continuing approximately 2/3 of the way through the upper left quadrant. Then, ease the line around in a gentle curve, ending at Point 1. From Point 1, ease the line downward in a gentle curve to meet Point 3. From Point 3, the line runs straight to the bottom right hand corner of the rectangle, ending at point 6.

To determine Point 4, draw a line that is perpendicular (90 degrees) to the straight line running from Point 5 to Point 2. Beginning at Point 6, draw a line perpendicular to the straight line running between Point 3 & Point 6, as shown in the "Moccasin Pattern" illustration on the facing page. These two lines should intersect on the centerline of the rectangle, determining Point 4. The line from Point 4 up to through the center will be the "T" opening when the moccasin is completed. The top of the "T" is cut on the center line and it should be between 1½" - 2" wide.

Cut out the upper pattern, including the "T", and apply some tape at the corners of the "T" cuts to prevent them from tearing while you test the fit. Drape the paper pattern over your foot to see how well it fits, and since it is only paper now, it can be adjusted for length and width at this time. The pattern should touch the floor all the way around with about a ¼" overlap which allows for the turn under when attaching the sole. Make sure it fits before cutting out the leather!

The next step is sometimes the most difficult since you have to cut into that beautiful hide! There are important considerations, or "tricks of the trade", when deciding how to lay out the uppers on the hide. When using brain tanned hide, note that there is a smoother side of the hide (the hair side) and a rougher side (the "meat" or inside). Beadwork is normally done on the smooth, or hair side.

The prime part of the hide is associated with where the premium cuts of meat come from. The first choice is the rump area, which is the larger area above the tail of the hide. Other choices are up toward the neck, staying along the center. The neck area is thicker and tougher to work with, but it can also be used. Try to avoid the thin, belly area which is located approximately midway along the outer edges of the hide. Wherever you choose to cut the uppers from, make sure you place them side-by-side and running lengthwise along the hide! Do not place them end to end. Remember that hide stretches differently at different locations so to make them match, they should be laid out on opposite sides of the center line of the hide.

Tape the "T" closed on the upper pattern, lay it out on the hide and trace around it. Move it to the opposite side and trace it again, remembering to flip it over, as you don't want two right or two left feet!

Fig. 3

Craftwork Techniques

Fig. 4

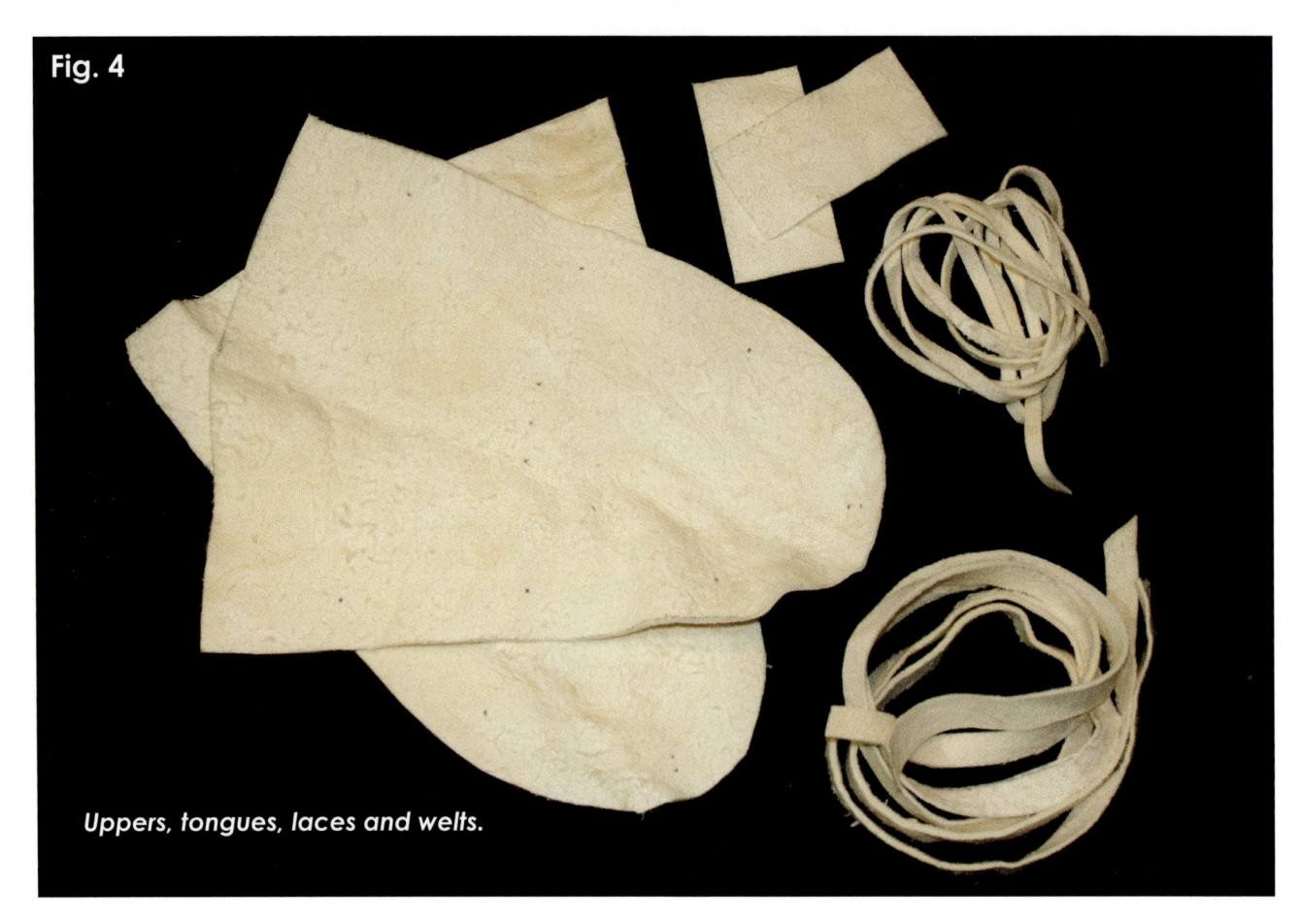

Uppers, tongues, laces and welts.

Once your upper pattern has been traced onto the buckskin, use the large, sharp scissors to cut it out. Begin at the bottom corner of the upper and cut up around the toe and back down to the heel, leaving approximately 1" of extra leather extending back past Point 4, the heel mark. This will allow enough leather so that the welt, which is cut next, will be plenty long. Finish the upper by cutting the heel seam to Point 4.

Once this is completed, cut a 1/2" wide strip for the welt from along the edge of the remaining buckskin. The purpose of the welt is to protect the stitches, and although it is not required, it really helps make the moccasin last longer and look better, as well. I try to use thick hide for this, so if my upper hide is thin, I might cut the welts from a thicker area of the hide or even from a different one. Next, cut another strip approximately 1/8" wide for the lace. Repeat this entire process for the other upper, making sure that you cut out both a right and a left side. The tongues are the last pieces to be cut and they should be 2" wide by 3" long.

The last step before beginning the beadwork on the upper is marking the location of the designs. In this case, we are making Cheyenne style moccasins with 7 perimeter design elements. There will be one on the toe and three on each side. The toe design falls in between the big toe and the second toe, and the others are evenly spaced along the sides with the center design located at the arch.

You are now ready to begin the beadwork. The point at which this is begun is up to each craftsman, but I prefer to start at the center of the toe design. The reason for this is pretty simple, as the toe is the most difficult to complete. It is easier to make the necessary turns if you start in the center and work your way along both sides. There are several important things to keep in mind here. Since you have added about ¼" around the perimeter of the pattern, the beadwork must start ¼" back from the edge. It is also important to keep all of your knots on the outside of the upper, as these will be covered by the beadwork. The beading thread should not pass all the way through the hide, but should only catch the upper half of the thickness. Going all the way through the hide and placing the knots on the inside could cause them to weaken and come loose, so they are all under the beadwork on the outside of the hide.

Thread a Sharps needle with enough size "D" Nymo thread to double it. Then coat it with beeswax to keep it from getting tangled. I keep my beeswax handy, as I prefer to wax the thread every 5-7 stitches. I find it is best to wax lightly and more frequently rather than waxing more heavily one time. Tie a knot in the end of the thread and you are ready to begin beading. Start the needle at an angle about 1/2" from the edge of the leather and about 1/16" from the center. Remember to only go about halfway through the thickness of the hide rather than completely through! Bring your needle out at the center of the toe design, approximately 1/4" from the edge.

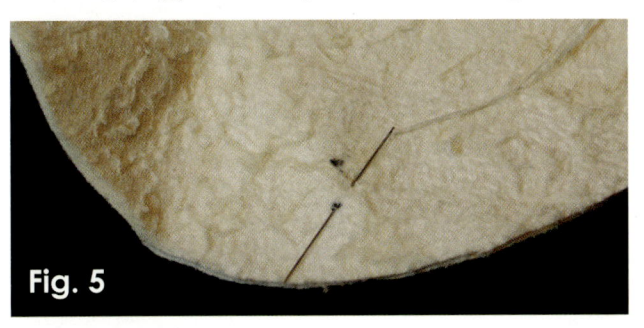

Fig. 5

For the first row of beadwork, put 8 beads on the needle, pulling them down to the end of the thread. Place them so that they lie on the hide leading towards the center of the "T". This 8 bead section determines the width of your lane of beadwork. *Note:* Check the relative sizes of all your bead colors. Even though you may have purchased all 11/0 size beads, some colors may run smaller than others! So make sure that this first row represents the average width of 8 beads. Make another stitch at the point where the width of 8 beads lies, coming out 1/2 bead width past this first row. This is the tricky part because if the stitch is too wide, it will pull the hide together, making the moccasins too small. If the stitch isn't tight enough, the hide will roll and the work will not lie flat.

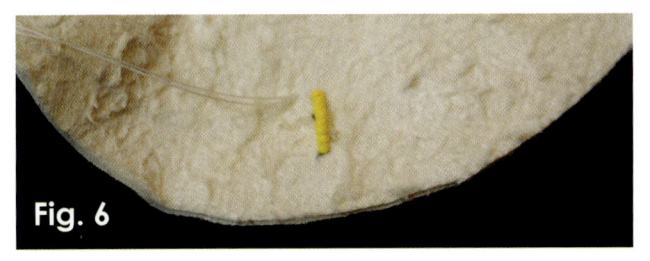

Fig. 6

The next row places another 8 beads alongside the first row, but because you are beading around the toe, the stitch at the outer edge of the upper is just a little bit wider than the stitch at the top, or inside of the row. This is shown in **Figure 6**. In the paragraph above, I explained that you should avoid taking a wide stitch because it will cause the hide to pull together; however, this is one of my secrets. I make the stitch slightly wider but only "snug" it up rather than pulling it tight, which keeps the hide from pulling together. Continue working your way around, making the bottom stitches slightly wider and snug, while making the top stitches normal width and tighter. Continue this technique for about 20 rows. Although this is one of the hardest techniques to learn, mastering it will make the rest of beading the moccasins a cinch!

After completing the toe design, tie off the thread by coming up from your last stitch in the center of a lane. Take a small stitch, running your needle through the loop that this forms, and pull it up snugly. Repeat this process by making another stitch that comes up through the leather, then clip off the excess thread. See **Figure 7**.

Fig. 7

To begin beading again with a new length of thread, knot the end and move down to the next design element. Once again, start in the center and bead back in the other direction so as to meet the first part of the toe design. Be sure to keep your lane straight and even, and 1/4" away from the outer edge. As you fill in the area between this design element and the toe element, your stitches may have to be slightly wider at the outer edge, as before. This simply depends on where you stopped. See **Figure 8**.

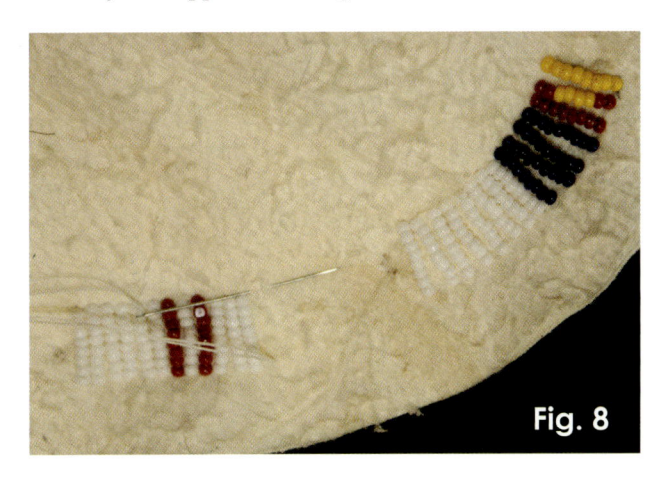

Fig. 8

99

Craftwork Techniques

Once you reach the point at which you stopped in the toe area, tie off the thread as explained above, making sure the knot will be covered by the beadwork and is not visible. Once again, begin beading at the center of the second design element, beading back toward the heel of the upper. This technique is used to center each design element along the first lane of beadwork.

Next, proceed to the design element at the instep and continue working along the edge on one side until all the design elements of this bottom row are completed. When this lane is completed, go back to the center of the toe and finish the lane down the other side using the same technique as you used on the first side.

After completing the first lane on one side, proceed to the other side. When the entire first lane of beadwork on this upper is completed, put it aside and then complete the first lane on the other upper.

I normally start in the center of the toe and work my way back toward the heel. The center row (which consists of the yellow beads in **Figure 11**) points toward the center of the "T" at the center of the moccasin. Remember that the bottoms of the 2nd, 3rd and 4th rows are all going to be wider than they are at the top. The top gets a little crowded, but this is necessary to make the beadwork curve around the toe correctly.

Next, bead the 2nd, 3rd and 4th lanes on each moccasin. This is an important point! As in other crafts, the tension you place on the beading thread can change as you progress. Further, the hide will stretch and give as you bead, and it is very important for both uppers to match. If you complete the beadwork on the entire first upper before starting the second, it is very difficult to make them match. So, do not be tempted to do this just to see what it will look like! Pick up the second upper, starting at the beginning as you did with the first one and continue until the perimeter beadwork on both uppers is completed. As you bead along the sides, make sure that each design element lines up with the one on the lane below it. When working on the arc, or inside, of the upper, you will find that the stitches, except those over the design, do not line up. This is because the inner side of each row of the upper is shorter than the outside. The background, of course, does not have to line up.

Fig. 9

Fig. 10

Fig. 11

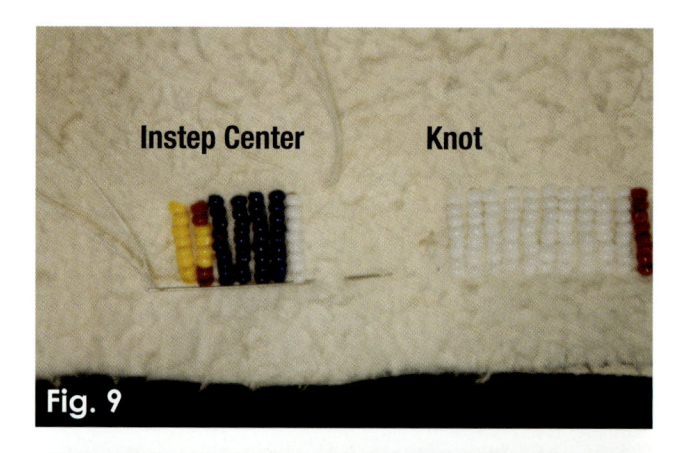

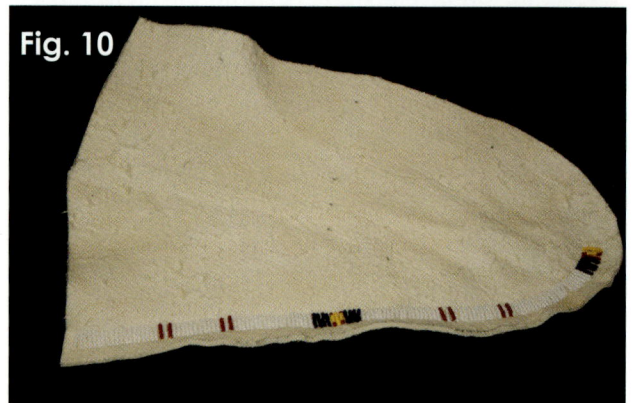

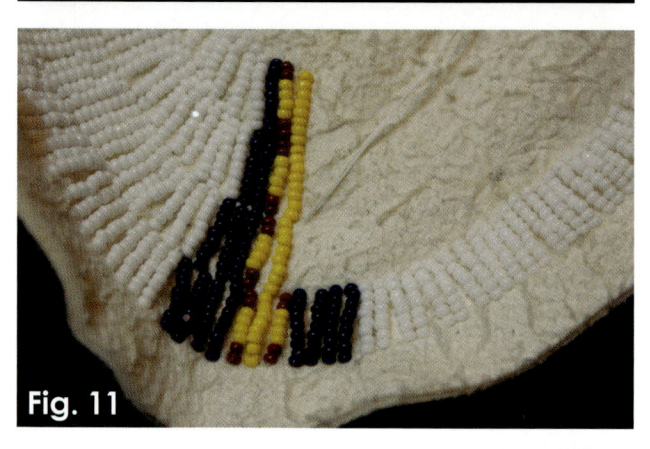

Fig. 12 *Thread behind the previous row.*

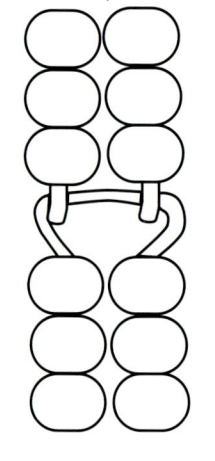

100

Fig. 13

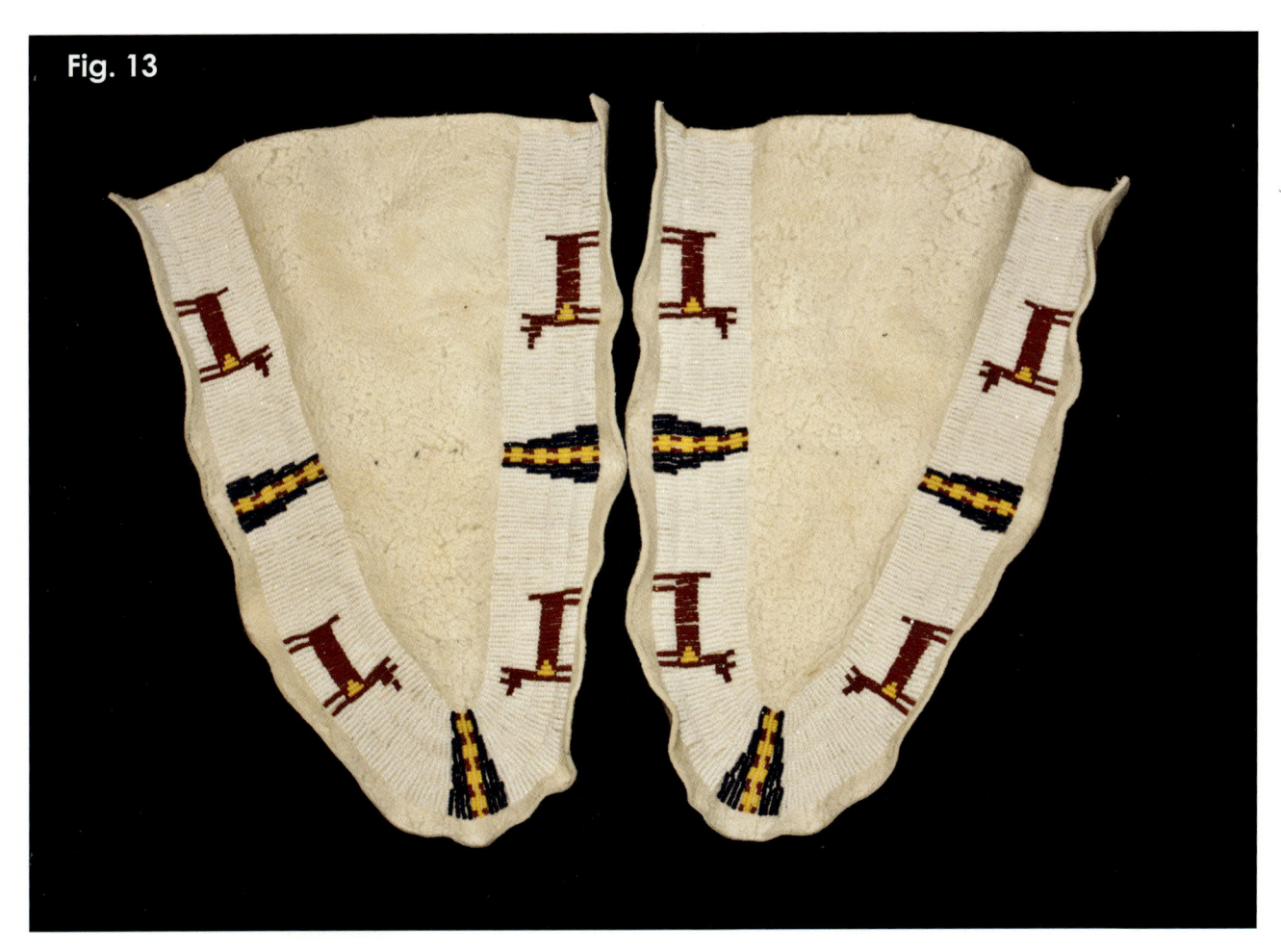

With this technique, it is important that your stitches only go partially through the leather. Another method is to catch the thread behind the previous row of beads, rather than going into the hide. This is illustrated in **Figure 12**. Personally, I do not prefer this technique as I feel it puts extra tension on the threads. Regardless of the technique you use, when the stitch is made, it should go slightly behind the previous row of beads.

The next step in the beading process is to bead the instep. The "T" makes the approximate line for this lane of beadwork, beginning 1/16" in from the line where the cut will be made. Draw a faint line with pencil to show the position of the edge of the row, then starting in the center, work your way out to each perimeter. Again, do both moccasin uppers at the same time, as this will keep the tension even from one moccasin to the other.

The next section to be beaded is the vamp area. Begin by choosing a design and deciding where it will be located. If your design is 4 rows wide, you will begin beading along the side of the center line, moving from the "T" to the perimeter toe design (**Figure 14**). If the design is 3 or 5 rows wide, mark a light, narrow line ½ row wide off the center line for a guide line to follow. See **Figure 15**. Another measurement needed is the position where the design will start. This should be in inches rather than in a number of rows. On this pair of moccasins, there are 3 bead lanes in the vamp design, so they require using the offset center line.

Fig. 14

Start in the center.

101

Craftwork Techniques

Starting at the point you marked for the vamp design, begin beading up toward the instep. Once you reach the instep, start again at the bottom of the design and bead down to the perimeter toe design. When you reach the perimeter toe design, the lane must be made narrower, so just use the correct number of beads necessary to fill in the gap.

Work from either side to fill in the rest of the beadwork on the vamp area. I normally start at the instep and complete the design elements first, working down toward the toe. When the design elements are completed, finish filling in the rows of background beadwork, which is white in this example. When the vamp area is completely filled in on the one side, finish the beadwork on the other side.

After completing the first moccasin, finish beading the other one. At this point, you could consider the moccasin beadwork complete; however in this example, more beadwork will be added on the flaps.

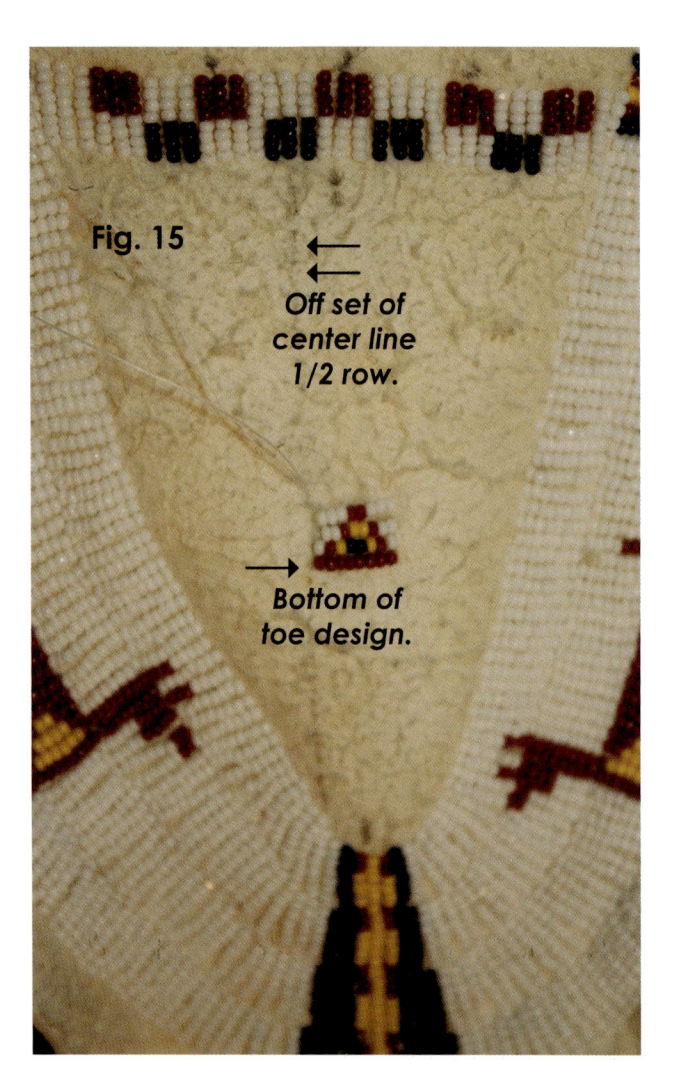

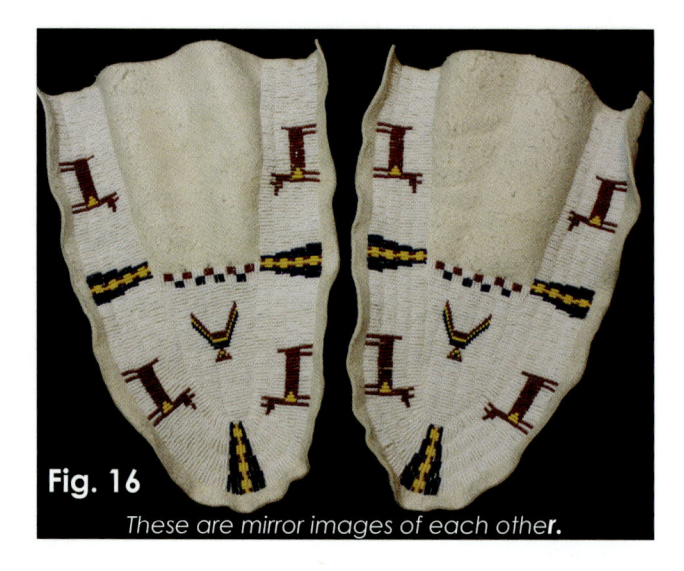

Fig. 16

These are mirror images of each other.

Before beginning the beadwork on the flaps, the "T" must be cut and the holes punched for the laces. Starting at the back of the upper, cut towards the middle and once you reach the instep, cut the cross section of the "T". Each side cut is about ¾" long, making the opening 1½" across.

Fig. 15

← ←
Off set of center line 1/2 row.

→ *Bottom of toe design.*

Fig. 17

On each upper, 4 sets of holes are required: 2 on each side at the rear, and 2 on each side of the instep just behind the "T". It is important that these holes are placed so that a lane of beadwork can be done over the top of them to cover both the holes and the lace that goes through them. This is shown in **Figure 18**.

Fig. 18

Fig. 21

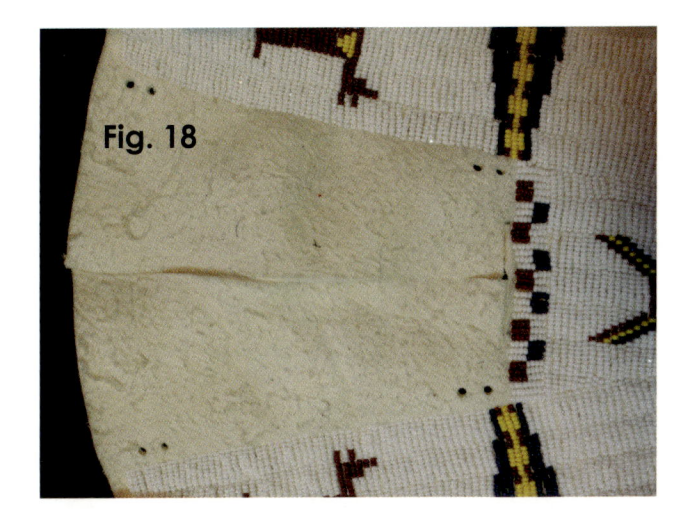

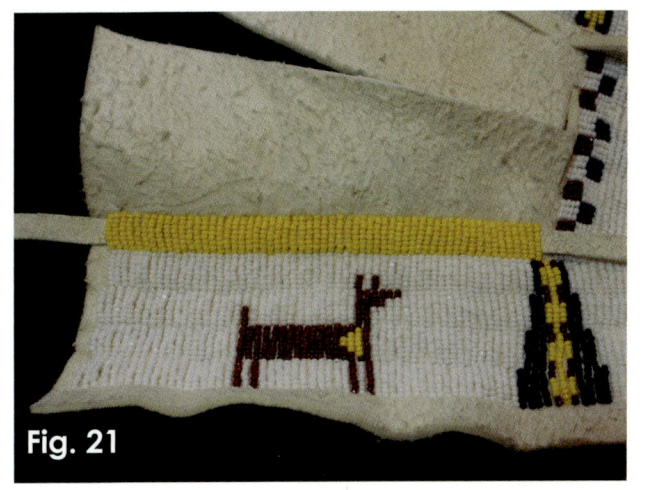

Now you can begin beading the flaps. The first lane covers the tie lace and is usually done in a solid color to accent the entire moccasin. This is beaded just as you would any other lane, except that the lace is in place and the bead rows cover it up. Make sure that there are no knots under the beadwork covering the lace, as wear and tear could cause them to fray and eventually break.

After the yellow "lace" lane is completed, bead the remainder of the flap. In this case, there are two more rows. Once this work is completed, trim the flap down to the edge of the beadwork, leaving about 1/8" of leather showing. Both sides should match, and now the beadwork is completed! Note: The flap can also be edge beaded, or if you prefer, it can simply be left plain.

Fig. 19

Fig. 22

Fig. 20

103

Craftwork Techniques

The next step is preparing the soles. Begin by tracing the outline of your foot on a piece of heavy paper such as a grocery bag or butcher paper. Stand barefooted on the paper and using a pencil held straight up and down, trace around your foot. Using this as a basic shape, draw the pattern so that the point of the sole falls between your great toe and your second toe. Draw a gentle curve around your other toes and down the outside of your foot to the heel area. The heel can be rounded or slightly squared off, as in the Cheyenne style. The inside of the pattern forms a straight line between your great toe and the outside edge of the heel.

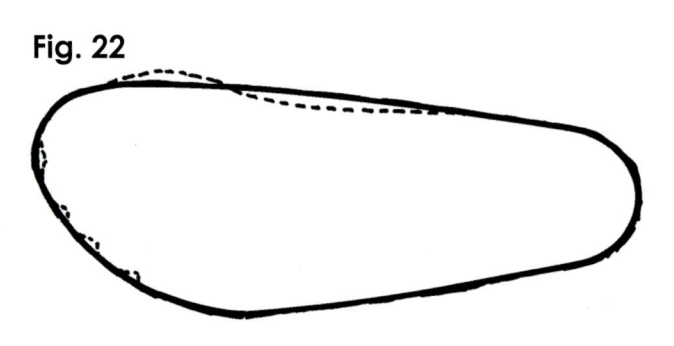

Fig. 22

Next, transfer the pattern to your sole material. This can be either rawhide or latigo leather, such as an oil or alum tanned (white) variety. Rawhide requires some special work, which I will explain; however, I prefer to use white latigo for my soles. Once you have traced your pattern onto the leather, cut out the soles using a pair of sharp scissors, such as the Gingher shears. This can be hard to cut, so it is best to do short sections at a time. You will note that the scissors are meant to cut in only one direction to get a straight up and down cut, so you must cut in a counter clockwise direction in order to cut cleanly.

Once the soles are cut out, you will pre-punch holes for attaching them. If you are using rawhide, it will need to be dampened in order to punch through it. Rawhide absorbs water, so you only want the soles damp and not ringing wet. One of the easiest ways to do this is to put them between wet towels overnight. Once damp, you can punch the holes in the same manner, regardless of whether you are using rawhide or latigo. A sharp awl is a must for this process, and I use a regular awl that has been ground down to a very sharp point.

Fig. 24

Starting at the toe, punch holes at an angle going through the inside (rough side) to the outside, coming out on the side of the sole as shown in **Figure 24**. If you punch holes straight up and down, the stitches will wear out, so coming out the sides protects the stitches. This is very important. Take care not to push the awl too far through the leather, as this can cause the hole to "rip" out. Carefully rocking your hand back and forth can help get the awl through the heavy hide. In the areas around the toe and heel, the holes should be spaced about 1/8" apart, while along the sides they can be spaced slightly farther apart. The toe and heel areas need tighter stitches than the sides, as they take higher stress. However, for the best results do not make the holes along the sides too far apart. **Figure 25**, shows the proper spacing.

Fig. 23

Fig. 25

Fig. 26

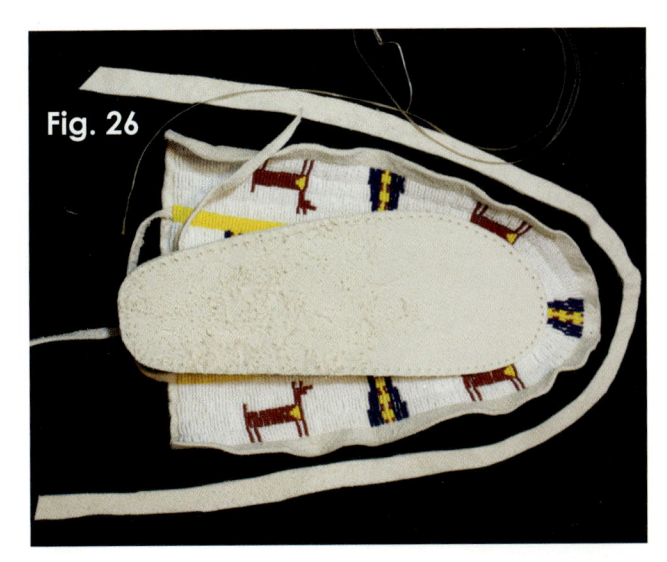

The purpose of the welt is to protect the stitches, and although it is not required, it really helps make the moccasin last longer and look better as well. I try to use thick hide for this, so if my upper hide is thin, I might cut the welts from a thicker area, or sometimes even from a different hide.

Assembly of the various pieces is next, after which the final touches, such as beading the heel seam, can be added. So, there is a bit more beadwork left to do!

In order to attach the uppers to the soles, lay out an upper, the welt that you cut from the same side, and the sole. This is done inside out, so if you are not sure which sole goes with which upper, lay the sole down with the rough side up. This will be the inside of the moccasin. Place the upper on top with the beadwork facing up, and in this way, you will know which upper matches which sole.

Next, lay the upper down with the beadwork facing up and the sole on top. Place the welt along the outer edge of the upper as shown in **Figure 26**. If you cut the welt as described earlier, it will be a little longer than the upper.

Mark the spot between the big toe and the second toe, marking both soles exactly the same. This marked point will line up with the center of the toe design.

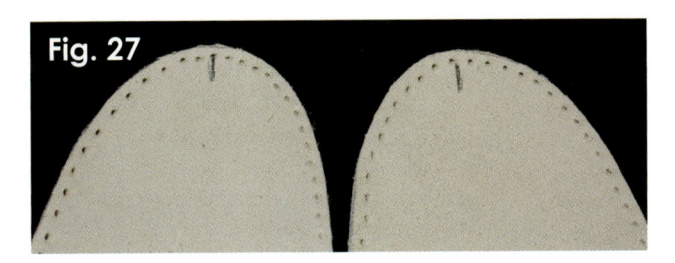

Fig. 27

I use a medium size, curved Glover's needle for attaching the sole, as it is better for this than a straight one. The curved area acts as a grip, providing some leverage which helps you push it through the leather. Be aware that Glover's needles are extremely sharp, with a 3-sided point like knife blades. It is not the poking of your finger that is the danger, rather it is the accidental running of the tip over a finger or hand. This will cut, burn and hurt! If you are using a straight Glover's needle, a pair of pliers is handy to help push the needle through the three layers of hide.

Thread the Glover's needle with simulated sinew that has been split in half. Do not split this any thinner, as it will be doubled. This should be about half again as long as the welt so that it will be long enough to sew the entire side.

Note: Genuine sinew can be used for attaching the soles, but this takes a little more time and effort. The sinew must be broken down and stripped apart, which I do by wrapping it in a dish towel and pounding it with a hammer. This breaks the fibers apart from their natural glue so you can pull off a piece of the required thickness. Sinew is much shorter than thread, so you will be working with short pieces of material.

Starting at the mark you made at the toe, insert the needle through the pre-punched hole in the sole. Then go through the welt about 1/8" in from the edge and then through the upper, about 1/8" from its edge and exactly at the center of the toe design. Note that the upper is on the bottom, and inside out at this time.

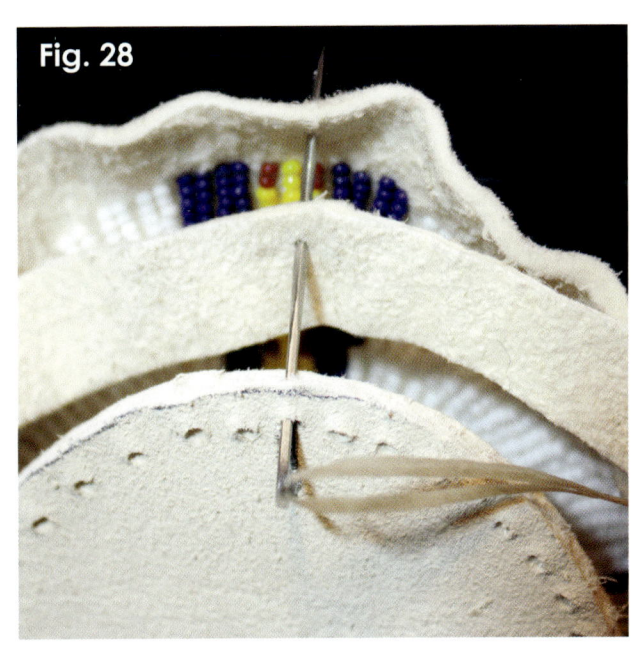

Fig. 28

Craftwork Techniques

As you pull the sinew through the leather, leave a tail about 2" long, but WITHOUT KNOTTING IT! If you put a knot here, it will always feel like there is a pebble in your shoe! Hold the tail down along the side and sew over it with successive stitches. Before continuing the stitching, examine the three pieces. The upper should be longer than the sole, and as you stitch the pieces together, you must "ease" the upper to match the sole. So with each stitch, you will cause the upper to pucker slightly, keeping the welt straight and all your stitches tight! Your goal is to have all the gathering done by the time you reach the instep area of the upper. Then from the instep back to the heel it should be straight. Mastering this technique may take some practice, but it does not have to be perfect here. Try to complete the gathering or "easing" by the time you reach the instep, which is the point where the "T" begins. If gathering reaches a little further than the instep, or even a little less, it is okay.

You should find it relatively easy to push the curved Glover's needle through the three layers of hide if the sole is pre-punched. Tighten each stitch, but be careful not to pull too tightly or you will rip out the pre-punched holes. If this happens, punch another hole very close to the ripped one and make the stitch, pulling it just snug. The sole will be slightly weakened at that point, so snug is not the same as tight! Once you reach the heel, back stitch around it to end the thread, as shown in **Figure 30**. This will give added strength to the heel portion where most of the wear and tension occurs on the moccasins.

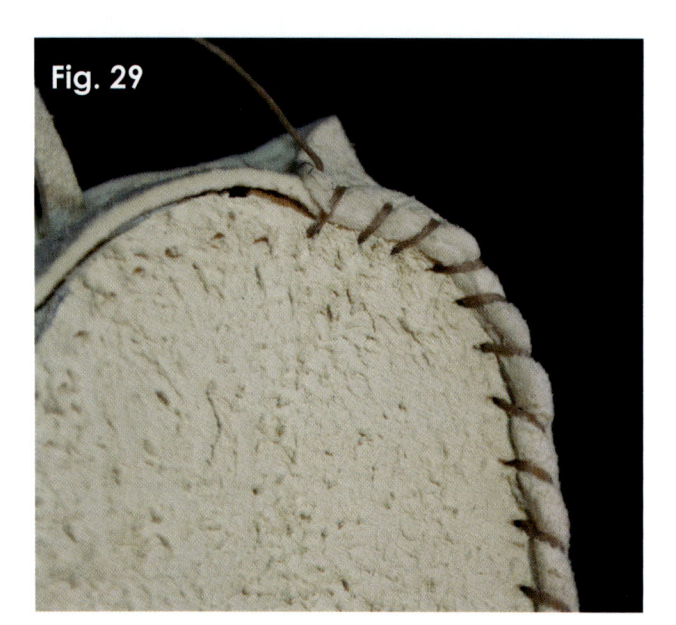

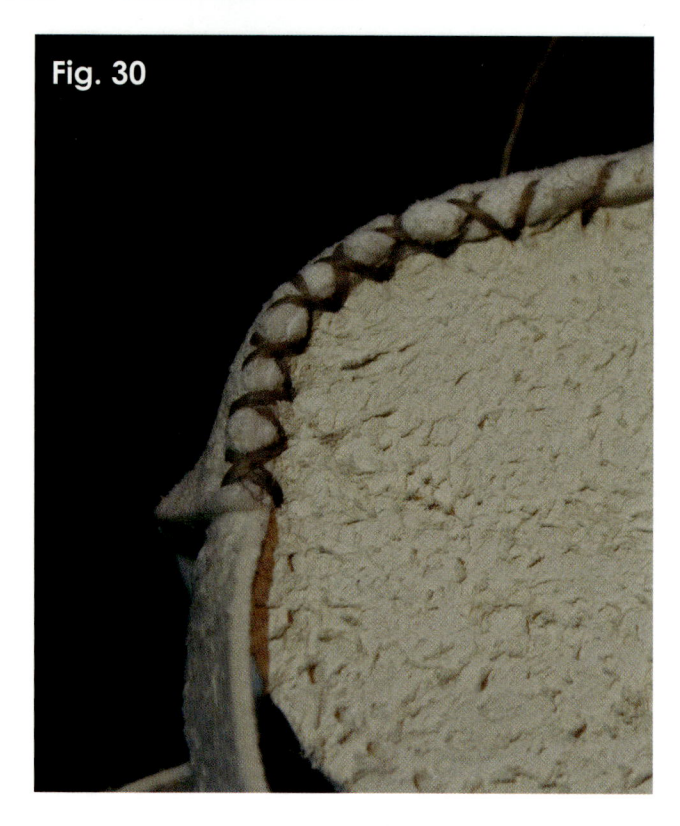

Fig. 30

Clip the welt and begin stitching down the other side of the sole. Repeat the same process, starting one hole away from the center so that the first couple of stitches will overlap each other. See **Figure 31**.

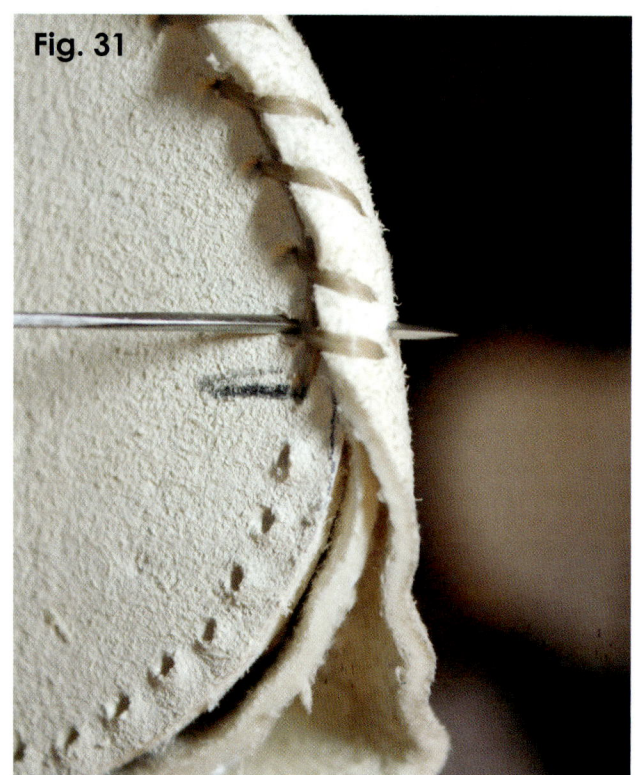

Fig. 31

Fig. 29

106

Moccasins

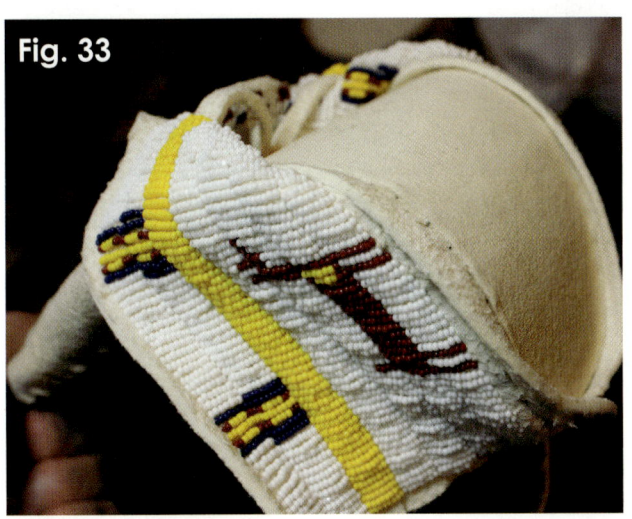

Fig. 32

Fig. 33

Fig. 34

Figure 32 shows how the moccasin will look once you have completed stitching the sole all the way around. Of course, you will have to repeat this entirely for the other moccasin, and then they will be ready to turn right side out.

The process of turning the moccasins is often one of the most difficult parts of making them. This is a slow and tedious process that is very hard on the hands (at least on mine), so take your time! Starting at the heel of the first moccasin, as shown in **Figure 33**, push it through to begin to turn it right side out.

The first part is easy, but as you reach the instep, it will begin to get harder. The photo at right shows how tight and pinched the mid-part of the vamp is. This is the most difficult section to turn, so you must push side-to-side from inside the upper and sole together. This is slow going, making very little progress at a time, but don't give up! Just keep pushing side to side as you work this part of the moccasin through to finish turning it.

Craftwork Techniques

As you move further down the vamp towards the toe, it will get a little easier. At this point, you need either very strong fingers or a smooth, rounded stick to do the pushing. I use my fingers and just keep pushing until soon, the entire toe just pops out. There; you finally made it! Now repeat the process on the other moccasin.

After both moccasins are turned right side out, trim the welt off close to the edge of the sole. Cut in a counter-clockwise direction if you are using right handed scissors, which will make a cleaner cut. Be careful you don't cut the stitches attaching the sole. Once trimmed, work the welt into the area between the upper and the sole, which will kind of fluff it up.

Next, you must sew up the heel seam. Use a small Glover's needle that is double threaded, with the thread heavily waxed. Starting at the bottom by the sole, stitch up the back using a "baseball" stitch, which helps to make the seam lie flat. Begin by knotting the end of the thread and inserting the needle from inside the moccasin. When the needle comes out, run it over the edge of the leather and back through the other side of the moccasin from the inside. Continue stitching in this manner, across from one side to the other, until you reach the top. This is illustrated in **Figure 35**. Once you reach the top, make three or four loop stitches to end the seam. Then cut the thread and pull the lace up snugly against the finished seam. Repeat for the other moccasin.

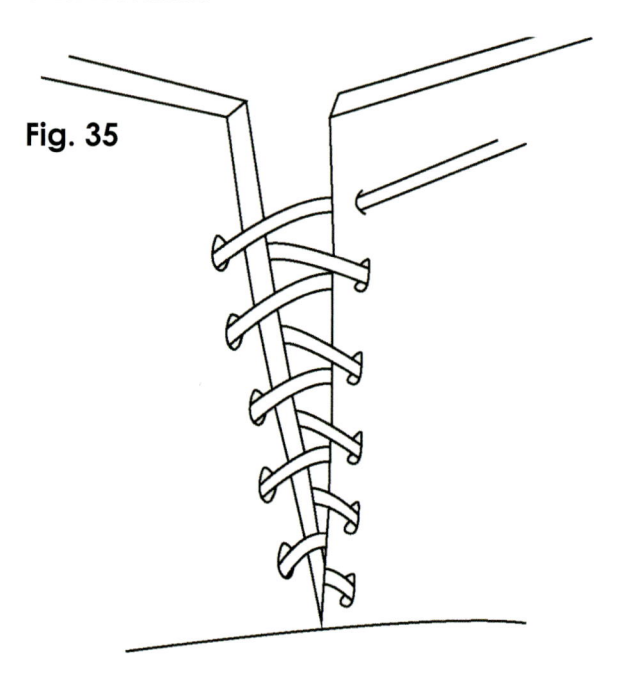

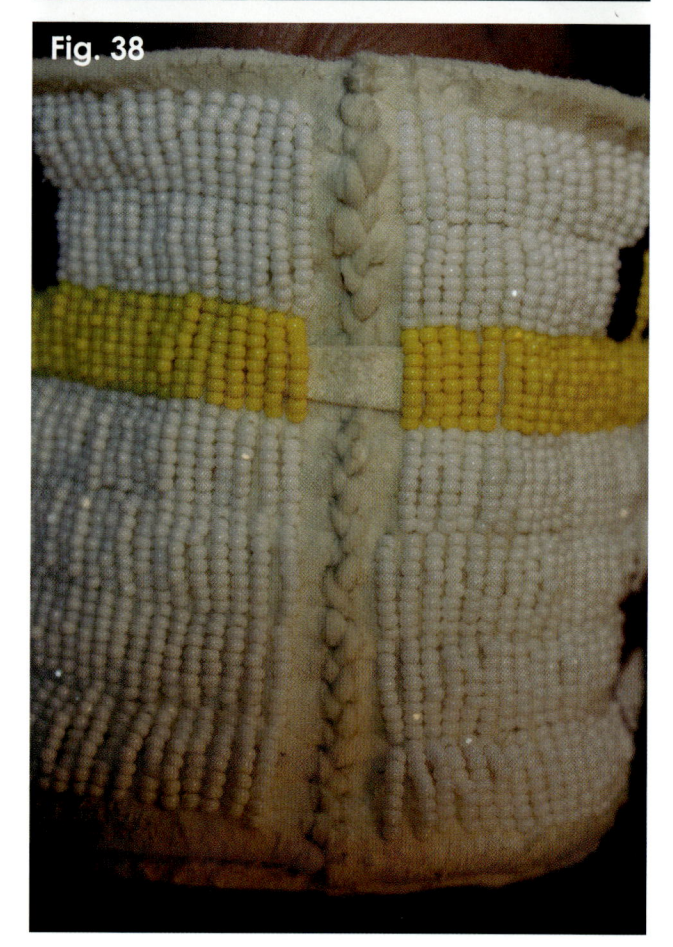

Fig. 36

Fig. 37

Fig. 38

Fig. 35

Moccasins

Fig. 39

Fig. 40

Fig. 41

Now is the time to apply the beadwork over the heel seam. Thread your beading needle as you did when beading the upper, and starting at the sole, add a lane of beadwork up the back and over the seam. See **Figures 39 & 40**.

The area where the lace crosses the line of vertical beadwork at the heel can either be beaded or left plain. If you choose to bead it, make sure you do not catch the lace in your stitching. Another option is to to bead over the lace with, in this case, yellow. Or you can simply leave it plain as shown in **Figure 40**.

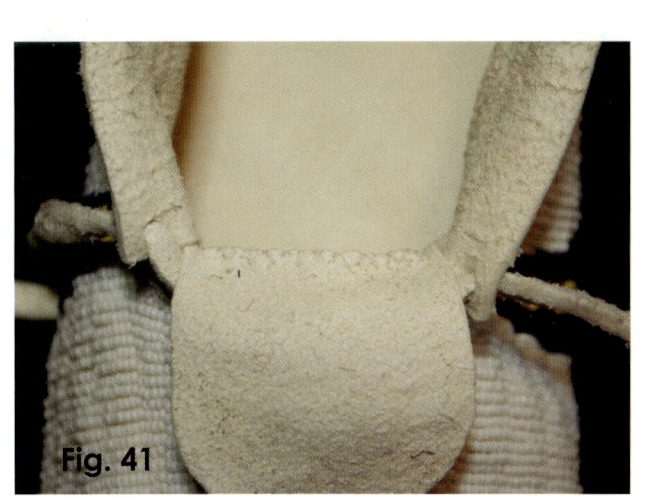

Using a small Glover's needle which is double threaded and heavily waxed, sew the tongues in place as shown in **Figure 41**, at right. Fold the back edge of the tongue over about ½", and with this folded edge toward the beadwork on the vamp, begin sewing it using a whip stitch. Sew completely across to the other side, then stitch back across to end the sewing. Trim the folded edge the same way you trimmed the welt, then trim the front of the tongue to the desired shape. In this case, it is rounded, but it can also be straight, V-shaped or tapered. It can also be beaded if desired, as this is simply a personal preference. As shown in **Figure 41**, punch a small hole in the top corner of each flap in order to form "eyelets" through which the laces run. Laces are typically criss-crossed and then tied in a bow to complete the moccasins. The completed moccasins are illustrated in **Figures 42-44** on the following page.

Craftwork Techniques

Fig. 42

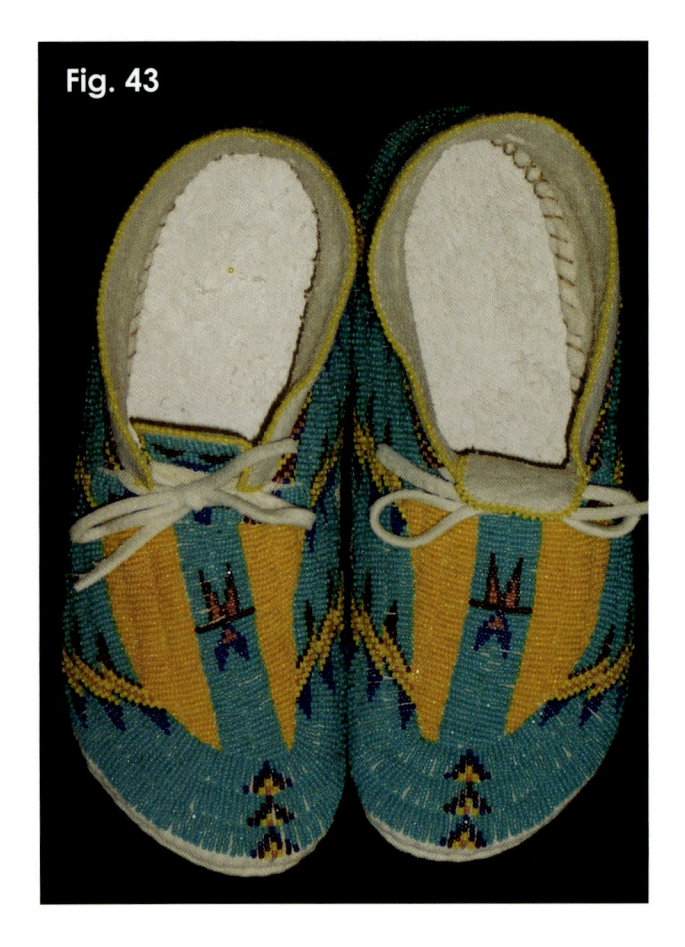

Fig. 45

Fig. 43

Fig. 46

110

References & Web Links

Many excellent books with full-color photographs and identification of various American Indian objects are available, as well as hundreds of excellent, on-line photographs from many major museums housing large collections of material. Some of the best are listed here but diligent internet searches will reveal many more. However, a word of caution is advisable, as many times tribal attributions were assigned by museums and collectors based on the tribe from which an item was collected. Due to trading, gifting and intermarriage, these are not always correct.

Craft Books:
American Indian Beadwork - Hunt & Burshears
Beads and Beadwork of the American Indian - William C. Orchard
Beadwork Techniques of the Native Americans - Scott Sutton
Beadworking With Today's Materials - Loren & Donna Woerpel
Focus on Feathers - J. Andrew Forsythe
Native American Beadwork - Georg J. Barth
Native American Moccasins - George M. White
Quill and Beadwork of the Western Sioux - Carrie A. Lyford
The Arapaho - Alfred Louis Kroeber
Traditional Indian Bead & Leather Crafts - Smith & VanSickle
Whispering Wind Craft Annuals (Vol. 2-8) - Jack Heriard, Ed.

Museum Collection Books:
A Persistent Vision - Richard Conn
American Indian Art - Norman Feder
Circles of the World - Richard Conn
Footsteps on the Sacred Earth: Southwestern Collection of The Bata Shoe Museum -
  Jill Oakes & Rick Riewe
Hau Kola! - Barbara A. Hail
Splendid Heritage: Perspectives on American Indian Art - John & Marva Warnock, Editors

Museums:
American Museum of Natural History (AMNH) - Washington, D.C.
  http://www.amnh.org/exhibitions/permanent-exhibitions/
  http://anthro.amnh.org/north
Bata Shoe Museum - Toronto, ON, CA
  http://www.batashoemuseum
Denver Art Museum - Denver, CO
  http://www.denverartmuseum.org/
National Museum of the American Indian (NMAI) - Washington, D.C.
  http://www.americanindian.si.edu/searchcollections/results.aspx?regid=341&sort=1

Magazines:
American Indian Crafts & Culture Magazine - Published by Tyrone Stewart, Tulsa, OK
Moccasin Tracks - Published by the California Indian Hobbyist Association
Whispering Wind Magazine - Published by Written Heritage, Folsom, LA
  http://www.writtenheritage.com/

Website Links:
American Museum of Natural History-
  http://anthro.amnh.org/anthropology/databases/north_public/north_public.htm
Arapaho Moccasins from the Museum & Research Center of the American Mountain Men -
  http://user.xmission.com/~drudy/mtman/html/skchbk02.html
Braintanning - www.braintan.com
Detroit Historical Society -
  http://detroiths.pastperfect-online.com/33029cgi/mweb.exe?request=keyword;keyword=moccasin; dtype=d
Heritage Auctions -
  http://historical.ha.com/?type=-AMERICANA.HA.COM
Infinity of Nations Exhibit - National Museum of the American Indian - New York, NY
  http://nmai.si.edu/exhibitions/infinityof nations/
Morning Star Gallery -
  http://www.morningstargallery.com/
Native American Technology and Art -
  http://www.nativetech.org/clothing/moccasin/detail/ute.html
Splendid Heritage (Moccasins & Clothing) -
  http://www.splendidheritage.com/

Fig. 47

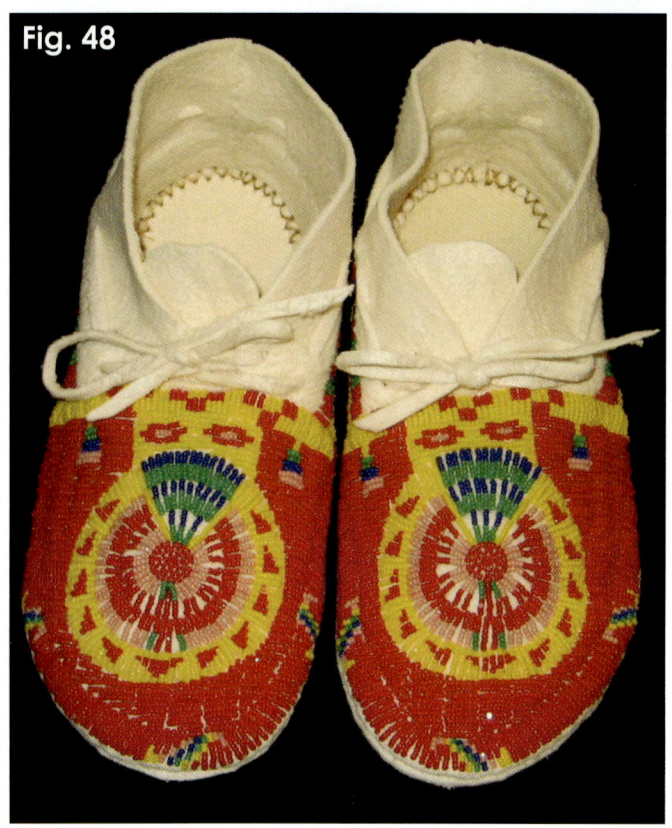

Fig. 48

Fig. 49

Fig. 50